SOUTH AFRICA

Joseph Jones, University of Texas

EDITOR

H. W. D. Manson

(*TWAS 220*)

TWAYNE'S WORLD AUTHORS SERIES

A Survey of the World's Literature

Sylvia E. Bowman, Indiana University

GENERAL EDITOR

TWAYNE'S WORLD AUTHORS SERIES (TWAS)

The purpose of TWAS is to survey the major writers —novelists, dramatists, historians, poets, philosophers, and critics—of the nations of the world. Among the national literatures covered are those of Australia, Canada, China, Eastern Europe, France, Germany, Greece, India, Italy, Japan, Latin America, the Netherlands, New Zealand, Poland, Russia, Scandinavia, Spain, and the African nations, as well as Hebrew, Yiddish, and Latin Classical literatures. This survey is complemented by Twayne's United States Authors Series and English Authors Series.

The intent of each volume in these series is to present a critical-analytical study of the works of the writer; to include biographical and historical material that may be necessary for understanding, appreciation, and critical appraisal of the writer; and to present all material in clear, concise English—but not to vitiate the scholarly content of the work by doing so.

(TWAS 320)

H. W. D. Manson

By CHRISTINA VAN HEYNINGEN and C. O. GARDNER

University of Natal

Twayne Publishers, Inc. :: New York

822
M289V

Preface

Of this book, two parts, the chapters on *The Festival* and on *Potluck*, have been written by Mr. C. O. Gardner, and the rest by me. This disproportion is mainly due to the fact that, having retired, I had the leisure, and Mr. Gardner had not. But Mr. Gardner has collaborated also in my share by listening to me read each chapter as I finished it and by making valuable criticisms and suggestions. He has also drawn up the chronology and the bibliography and has been kind enough to undertake most of the drudgery inevitable in preparing a manuscript for the press. For various facts about our author's life I am indebted to his mother, Mrs. D. Manson, and his elder brother, Mr. Leonard Manson, M.C.

A South African writing for the theater today must look forward to starvation unless he can contrive to alternate periods of earning a living in some other way with long spells of continuous and intense concentration on his writing. This Manson, being determined and tenacious, and no "hands-upper," managed to do. Professional theater hardly exists in South Africa except for the four provincial government-aided companies, for Cape, Free State, Natal, and Transvaal, and both it and the amateur theaters are interested mainly in box-office success. There is no Bantu theater at all. English-language drama has far less chance of success than Afrikaans. In Afrikaans the indigenous theater, apart from the excellent original plays by Uys Krige, his translations of Shakespeare, some translations by other people of Molière (highly popular and well done), Chekhov and Anouilh, and one or two fine poetic plays by N. P. van Wyk Louw, concerns itself largely, even at this date, with the Boer War. Serious English-speaking playwrights, on the other hand, are expected to write about nothing but the color question, and there has been nothing of real value on that subject, except perhaps the American musicals based on two of Alan Paton's novels, but these have not come to South Africa. His delightful short story, "Sponono," has also been successfully dramatized in this mode. A play or two of Guy Butler's has had glimpses of poetry and reality but no sustained depth; and Atholl Fugard has been much boosted, but in our opinion his work, about society's colored outcasts, is contemptibly feeble, false, dull, and undramatic. The interest of the color question is too soon exhausted, too unavoidably political, too narrow, and too fashionable a theme to have employed all of Manson's considerable energies of mind, though few men of our age had more capacity for understanding people of a different race from his own. Ambitious intellectuals among South African dramatists, whether English, like Atholl Fugard, or Afrikaans, have been trying to imitate the British theater of the absurd, and box-office comedies (amateur or professional) are usually imitations of London West End successes.

South African plays are hardly looked at overseas unless they exploit the fashionable color question. (How many people who ride that hobbyhorse are a thousandth part as much interested in its realities as Manson was?) Besides this, there is still a good deal of very deep unconscious English snobbery there (as well as in English-speaking Southern Africa) about "colonials." Your true-born Englishman simply cannot believe in his heart of hearts that any "colonial" can possibly be as good as an Englishman, let alone better! Nevertheless, as we relate elsewhere, Manson's work has been greatly admired by a few of the most eminent British actors and scholars of our time, two of his plays were produced in Britain, others had been accepted in Britain, America, and Canada, where one had been broadcast and options bought on others. All the plays, by the way, have been staged or broadcast, or both, in South Africa.

The critical method we employ in this book, which has been at least half consciously and often wordlessly employed by all good readers of literature from time immemorial, is that specifically initiated by Dr. F. R. Leavis, Dr. I. A. Richards, Mr. R. G. Biaggini and others, and adumbrated by Stephen Potter in his very interesting book, *The Muse in Chains*—that is, the method of "Practical Criticism." Assuming (what surely ought to be axiomatic) that the important thing about a work of literature is the book itself—not the author's life and ideas, not what people think of his work, what trends it reflects, and all the rest of it, but the book itself and the impact it makes in its living wholeness upon a qualified reader—we have devoted nearly all our attention to giving those people who have read Manson not at all, or only partially, or have forgotten what they have read, a *living* idea of each play we discuss. In other words, we have tried to make it, though at second hand, enter "alive into the heart," as Wordsworth says poetry should. With this purpose in mind, we have quoted as much as there was room for, commenting on what each quotation achieves and how it does so, and we have tried to tell the story in such a way as to approach, as nearly as possible, the effect made by the original play, and to make our summaries include as much interpretation and implied criticism as possible. In this attempt we hope we have not been altogether unsuccessful, and we hope that it will lead the uninitiated and the partly initiated to acquire and read Manson's plays for themselves and that it will inspire producers to give these plays, by means of first-rate productions, something of the fullness of life that they were created for.

C. v. H.

Acknowledgments

We have to thank the publishers for permission to quote from Manson's plays: A. A. Balkema, of Cape Town and Amsterdam, for *The Festival;* Human and Rousseau, of Cape Town, for *The Green Knight, Captain Smith,* and *The Noose-Knot Ballad;* Nasionale Boekhandel, of Parow, for *The Magnolia Tree* and *Pat Mulholland's Day;* and the University of Natal Press, of Pietermaritzburg, for *The Counsellors* and *Potluck.* For their services we wish to thank our typists, Mrs. Hill and Mrs. Patzer, and for criticism and encouragement, Mr. and Mrs. Jonathan Crewe.

We also wish to thank *Theoria* for permission to reprint *Unposted Letter* and the prologue to *Pat Mulholland's Day.*

Contents

Chronology

1926 Harley Manson born on January 29, at Tabora, Tanganyika (now Tanzania).

1931 Attends infant school at Dar-es-Salaam.

1933 Family moves to England. Manson later attends school at Chatham House, Ramsgate.

1939 Move to South Africa.

1940 Attends school at Saint Andrew's College, Grahamstown.

1944–1945 Serves with the Royal Natal Carbineers in Italy.

1946 Becomes a student at the University of Witwatersrand, Johannesburg.

1950 Writes *The Fight at Finnsburgh*.

1951 Temporary lecturer at the University of Natal in Pietermaritzburg. Writes *The Green Knight*. Marries Margaret Evans.

1953 Tours Europe. Writes *The Noose-Knot Ballad*.

1954 Lecturer at the University of Stellenbosch.

1955 Writes *The Counsellors*. *The Green Knight* produced at the University of Natal, Pietermaritzburg.

1956 *The Noose-Knot Ballad* produced at the Cygnet Theatre, Pietermaritzburg.

1956–1957 Writes *The Festival*.

1957–1958 Writes *Captain Smith*.

1958 Lecturer at the University of South Africa, Pretoria.

1960 Writes *The Magnolia Tree*.

1962 Lecturer at the University of Natal, Pietermaritzburg. *The Noose-Knot Ballad* produced by the Canadian Broadcasting Corporation.

1963 Writes *Pat Mulholland's Day*. Awarded the Olive Schreiner

Prize. *The Magnolia Tree* produced by the South African Broadcasting Corporation.

1964   *The Counsellors* produced at the University of Natal, Pietermaritzburg. *Pat Mulholland's Day* produced by the Iscor Dramatic Society, Pretoria. Awarded the Hofmeyr Prize.

1965   Visits England on an Ernest Oppenheimer travel grant. Writes *Potluck*. *Pat Mulholland's Day* produced by the South African Broadcasting Corporation.

1966   *The Magnolia Tree* produced at the Royal Lyceum Theatre, Edinburgh. *Captain Smith* produced by the South African Broadcasting Corporation.

1967   *The Magnolia Tree* published in the international theater magazine, *Gambit*. Writes *Magnus*. Marries Eleanore Kriener. *Potluck* produced (by Manson himself) at the University of Natal, Pietermaritzburg.

1968   *The Festival* produced at the University of York, England. Birth of a daughter, Kirsten.

1969   Killed in a road accident on May 29.
        Magnus produced at the University of Natal, Pietermaritzburg.

1970   Manson Memorial Fund established. Simultaneous publication of *The Counsellors, The Festival, Magnus* and *Potluck*.

1971   *Karl Gunter Hoffmann* published.

CHAPTER 1

Tone of Voice

I *South Africa Today*

ALL English South Africans, like the subject of this book, belong to at least two civilizations, that of Britain and that of South Africa. The present South African government detests this fact and is using every device of propaganda to make these South Africans renounce their British loyalties. But their British heritage is invaluable to most of them; and strongly as Manson, for example, objected to much government policy—especially that which discriminates against individuals on grounds of color alone or interferes with education—he would have freely admitted that he owed much to South Africa, and was glad to live in it.

English South Africans inherit from Britain mainly the great imaginative literature of the past, huge and varied as it is, and the values our British ancestors taught us. Shakespeare belongs to us as much as to any Englishman; so do Chaucer, Milton, Wordsworth, Lawrence, and the rest; we have been reading the great eighteenth- and nineteenth-century novelists all our lives, as well as the popular novelists of Edwardian and Georgian times and later, and our ideas of greatness and of virtue are based largely on the imaginary characters they have created and on the real ones of British history and biography. When we go to London for the first time we recognize parts of it as if we had been there before, and the names of streets there are often more familar to many of us than the houses in the small South African villages where we spent our childhood. Our imaginations are thoroughly accustomed to gray days, dark winters, mist, fog, perpetual rain, and deep ice and snow.

Yet we live in a very different kind of country, huge and still comparatively empty, but not long ago much emptier and wilder. Large tracts of it are very dry, and it is nearly always full of sunshine everywhere; it is peopled, where it is peopled, by human

15

beings, black, white and coloured,* whose lives and natures differ
greatly from those of the British. Life was very rough for everybody here not long ago, and people were hardy; and everything is
not yet tamed and subdued even for the whites. The landscape
nearly everywhere—whether flat and endless, like the Karoo or
Free State, or mountainous like the Western Cape, the Basutoland
or the Drakensberg border, or the Eastern Transvaal—is vast,
wild, and beautiful. Even the green part of Natal, which in summer is greener than Ireland and almost as fertile as the tropics, is
still comparatively wild; so that when we go to England, the very
trees look civilized to us, as ours do not. The sky here is very high:
immense heights of blue air stretch endlessly above us, and clouds
are as huge as continents. Both at night, when the stars are very
bright, and by day, one can, in most parts of the country, posi-
tively see the round earth moving in space, and see how fast it
seems to roll away from the sun by day. The stars in their constel-
lations wheel past at night as a stationary train seems to rush past
a moving one. On the thoughtful mind this kind of landscape has
a profound effect—the kind of effect very subtly and beautifully
suggested by Tolstoy in *War and Peace*, when he is reporting a
long questing discussion between Pierre and Prince André about
God and a future life. They are standing on the bank of a river,
and Tolstoy concludes the passage as follows:

Prince André did not reply. The carriage and horses had long been
led out on to the further bank, and were already harnessed, the sun
was half-sunken beneath the horizon, and the evening frost was beginning to incrust the little pools on the shore with starry crystals,
while Pierre and André, to the astonishment of the servants, coachmen
and ferry-men, still stood in the boat talking.
If God and the future life exist, then truth and virtue exist; and
man's highest happiness consists in striving for their attainment. One
must live, said Pierre, one must love, one must believe that we live
not merely now on this patch of earth, but that we have lived and
shall live eternally there in the universe. He pointed to the sky.
Prince André stood leaning on the rail of the ferry-boat and listening to Pierre. He never moved his eyes, but gazed at the red reflection
of the sun in the dark-blue flood. Pierre ceased speaking. All was

* In South Africa this word means of mixed blood, with some white
blood.

silent. The ferry-boat lay drifted along the bank, and only the ripples of the current could be heard lapping feebly against its sides. Prince André fancied that this patter of the water babbled a refrain to Pierre's words, "That is sooth, accept it: that is sooth, accept it." *

The passage suggests powerfully, yet by the most delicate means, the effect of the landscape upon the two men. They are both absorbed in a deeply serious and thoughtful discussion that is quite untouched by the trivialities of everyday life. It is not the kind of subject that would be likely to crop up on a street pavement in the middle of Birmingham, for example, nor is the mood in it the kind of mood that would be likely to possess two men in such circumstances. They would probably argue and score debating points. But, " 'there in the universe' [says Pierre]. He pointed to the sky"; and Tolstoy makes us feel that these two men are indeed surrounded, not by mere land and sky, but, almost visibly, by the whole vast inexplicable universe and by whatever mysterious force or spirit it is that informs it. This presence cannot be ignored: wherever the two men cast their absent glance, it is there, and part of its being silently enters deep into their souls. It is not like an African landscape: such details, with their strange wintry sadness, as, "the evening frost was beginning to incrust the little pools on the shore with starry crystals," or, "he never moved his eyes, but gazed at the red reflection of the sun in the dark-blue flood," make us feel vividly its cold Northern and Russian quality. But, like Africa, the landscape is essentially vast and wild and empty, a landscape in which mundane concerns are apt to drop away from the thoughtful mind, and where it seems unnatural to deny the kind of knowledge that the current "lapping feebly against the sides of the ferry-boat" seems to utter.

II *Language and Emotional Coloring*

From Britain Manson has been fortunate enough to inherit the great tradition of literature: poetry, drama, history, and novel. He is, in fact, very much more a part of it than any well-known British-born playwright or novelist I know of writing in England today. But he has spent most of his life in this great, thinly populated, untamed continent of Africa. This is partly, I think, what

* Translation from R. Bridges' anthology *The Spirit of Man*.

has made it impossible for him to fall into the arid nihilism of
successful plays like *Waiting for Godot,* or the blinkered domestic
dullness and squalid pettiness, and the sterile insincerity of the
Kitchen Sink school. A profound awareness of the infinite life of
"unknown modes of being" in which our little world is suspended
pervades all his plays and is most explicit in the very beautiful
Prologue to *Pat Mulholland's Day:*

> Now that you are settled and still,
> The house lights doused and dim,
> Make your minds like this dim darkness
> And bring up into it the smallest speck,
> The tiniest mote or atom it can think of—tip and touch
> And yet hold some memory of so doing—
> And imagine it
> Spinning and spinning in empty space.
> Then say this spinning speck
> Is our whole world—in one perspective.
>
> Ridiculous that it should spin
> Being flung off so long ago
> From another star or other speck
> That still is spinning, I suppose, somewhere—
> Or exploded—long ago—gone—
> In a silent white blast we never heard
> Or ever shall see,
> Although that blast may be
> What will blow our world away one day.
>
> Yet this day our little world still spins . . .
> Magnify this mote or speck and what do we see?
> It is dark on the one side away from the sun,
> Silver bright, it seems, on the other,
> And spinning and spinning continuously . . .
>
> And on that mote or speck are men—millions of them—
> Infinitesimal animals—
> Who crawl upon its surface and cling
> To life and this atom as it spins
> Through day and night
> Dark and light
> And life and death
> In a day, so to say—ridiculous!

Ridiculous to live at all
On such a tiny spinning ball!

But these are words, mere words . . .
Let's zoom our minds down, say, in human focus and feel;
Know and feel and see
Our huge, majestic world reel slowly through centuries,
And the great and glorious sun come up slowly,
And the distant, vast hills begin to loom,
Soar and assume dark shapes and sharp edges
Against the pale pink of the sky,
And the high peaks run down in ridges
To the wet, dark, silent valleys below,
Where nothing yet can be known but noises,
Running water and the croak of frogs.

But the world turns,
And pink pales slowly to pearly gold.
And rivers run not nowhere now,
And no longer only murmur in darkness
As if they'd lost their way;
We see.

We see reed beds dimly swaying and dark rocks,
And how the river mist lifts and curls.
As rose to pale gold lost,
So pale gold now to other lightness lifts,
And clouds all mackerel green and grey
Stay steady like a painted scene,
While the clear light of morning blue is set
That declares the scene is day.
What sort of day has dawned for this man
Whom we shall see presently behind this curtain?
Nothing is certain but that dawn begins
And night ends day.
And who among us shall see the next dawn certainly
No man can say.

The first stanza, with its slow and quiet rhythms as we read, and no doubt even more as we hear it in the crowded theater, acts upon us almost immediately like a kind of calming hypnosis. Our minds grow still, our restless bodies settle quietly, all worldly and irrelevant thoughts sink away; and, in that "dim darkness", we see what the poet tells us to see—the tiny speck (and how intensely his words make us realize its extreme smallness): ". . . the smallest speck / The tiniest mote or atom it [the mind] can think of—tip and touch / And yet hold some memory of so doing—." The minute speck is "our whole world," spinning senselessly (it seems) in a meaninglessly accidental universe. The next stanza, with its casual-sounding language and unponderous but not indifferent rhythm, reinforces the sense created here of the apparent purposelessness of the universe, reminding us, almost carelessly, that our world is doomed like all the other worlds that have perished before it.

The tone here is miles away from that of the self-pitying young writers of Britain today—the Osbornes and Becketts, the Weskers and Pinters of the modish theater. Manson quietly accepts the fact that our world is doomed. It is, simply, a fact—one of those facts that we have to accept because we have no alternative. Manson indulges in none of the fashionable heroics, no fulminations against God and those who brought us into the world, no stiff upper lip. He merely mentions the fact, emphasizing its queerness from the human point of view.

In the third and fourth stanzas he brings us nearer to the spinning ball. It looks much larger now but still ridiculously unimportant; it seems quite absurd that the millions of swarming, infinitesimal creatures that crawl upon its surface should so feverishly "cling / To life and this atom"—and for so ludicrously short a period: "Ridiculous to live at all / On such a tiny spinning ball!" The smilingly thoughtful, light, spinning rhythm seems to "throw away" the absurdity of it, implying, "It is not tragic; it is not even important."

But in the next three stanzas, as, at the poet's behest, we "zoom our minds down, say, in human focus and feel; / Know and feel and see," by a few vivid touches, he makes us powerfully feel that, true as all this is in a nonhuman perspective, to us it is "words, mere words"; and, as we go on, the compelling power of the poetry makes us realize with wonderful intensity and delight that the purposelessness of it all is utterly unimportant: it is life itself that matters, and it matters overwhelmingly. Now the language paints an entirely different picture from that of the first four stanzas—a picture all the truer because the one *they* paint is true too; we find ourselves stirred, and deeply, unexpectedly moved by the very coexistence of the beauty and importance of life with its insignificance and extreme fragility as it hangs suspended so precariously in the inconceivable infinite.

Manson achieves this here, in the Prologue, by describing, with the peculiar, delicate, intensely lively and tender vividness of which he is capable, the gradual dawn that is to begin Pat Mulholland's Day. The Prologue sets Pat in his eternal setting in the midst of the unimaginable universe of which he is a part, and to which, in a way, he gives a meaning. The play makes one feel that meaning. It *can* be *felt*, though, of course, never at all defined; it can be felt strongly when, in the play, we are made to bathe for awhile, as it were, in reality, the kind of reality that a poet creates, which, though not the same thing as life, nor a substitute for it, makes us much more alive to the actual that we can never fully know.

The Prologue has its own important function in the play by making us thrillingly aware of the wonderful nonhuman life in the midst of which our human lives are set. It may all be blown away one day, "in a white blast," but in the meantime the rhythmic movement of the pre-dawn light and the shapes of the mountains growing clearer in it are grand and glorious; the changing light and color as the earth "reels slowly" toward day are lovely beyond all speech; and there is something, Manson makes us feel, wonderfully touching and exciting in the multitudinous small life going on in the darkness of the valleys: "The wet, dark, silent valleys below,/Where nothing yet can be known but noises,/Running water and the croak of frogs." In the last stanza come the full dawn and the day, which is to show us Pat Mulholland, and to be his last.

The first scene is to open in his studio—he is a sculptor—very early in the morning, when he has just begun to dress. And the last words of the Prologue make us feel suddenly, peculiarly, poignantly anxious for him. We guess that the story will be a moving one, as indeed it is. The whole Prologue that has set the life on this planet so feelingly against the background of eternity has not diminished its importance but has made us realize it with remarkable force of conviction. For as Mrs. Blaiberg put it, the wife of the man who, at the moment of writing, was the world's longest-surviving heart-transplant patient: "The uncertainty of living makes you glad to be alive. Each morning when he wakes, he says 'Oh lovely! Another day'" As the Prologue comes to an end we are already deeply engaged in this one particular life which we had never heard of till this moment: it is already very much our concern:

> What sort of day has dawned for this man
> Whom we shall see presently behind this curtain?
> Nothing is certain but that dawn begins
> And night ends day.
> And who among us shall see the next dawn certainly
> No man can say.

III *Poetic Qualities*

The poem is typical of Manson's work at its best in that it all quivers with delicate life—delicate and yet strong and deep, the poet's imaginative intelligence being concerned with ultimates, just as the Tolstoy passage is. This too, in its very different mode, has a largeness, a deep seriousness of spirit in it. And it is of this age; for example, the consciousness of scientific discovery is one of the constituents of its lifeblood. The language, too, is the spoken language—the undebased language—of today. Manson is, as Wordsworth says all true poets are, "a man like other men"; his language is "the language actually used by men,"—used by men, not by the advertisers, journalists, and best-selling novelists who exploit the resources of language in order to sell their writing: and not by the cerebral poetasters, with their "strangulated utterance" and their search for images that will make them appear original yet "with it," or "literary" yet Laurentian, or otherwise cast what they regard as a flattering light on their own personalities. A man on the other hand "speaks with [his] own voice"; his sole concern is to make others see exactly what he means. He is not afraid, as so many modern writers seem to be, of "being caught out." Consequently he is direct, natural, and simple. It is certainly possible, though perhaps unusual, for a very simple and naïve adult person to be direct, natural, and simple. For a complex and sophisticated one, especially nowadays, it is a high achievement, both intellectual and moral.

And when, in poetry, this kind of simplicity is combined with— to use an old-fashioned and discredited word—poetic "magic," it cannot fail to give intense delight. Let us briefly consider one component of the so-called magic, its rhythm, by examining a small fragment of it: "Let's zoom our minds down, say, in human focus and feel; / Know and feel and see / Our huge, majestic world reel slowly through centuries." . . . The great grand movement of it, and our marvelous expanding vision, exulting in what is happening, are felt in the movement of the lines. "And the great and glorious sun come up slowly, / And the distant, vast hills begin to loom, / Soar and assume dark shapes and sharp edges." . . . The rhythm expands with the glory of the revelation; our sense of its majesty grows as the words create the scene; and as, step by step, light and sight grow clear, that half-unnoticed rhyme in the middle of the line, "loom-assume," makes us aware of something formal happening here that gives the whole movement added grace and power.

Manson's management of dramatic verse reminds one of the student's comment on the balcony scene in *Romeo and Juliet*. "It is so beautiful," she wrote, "that it is almost poetry." This naïve statement is one of the finest compliments ever paid to Shakespeare's dramatic verse. On the speaker, it unconsciously implied, the scene has had the full effect that poetry with all its devices of sound and rhythm is meant to have, and yet the dialogue was so entirely natural that she had not realized that any devices were being used. This is exactly what T. S. Eliot in his famous essay on dramatic verse said he himself was trying to achieve. In passages like this one from the Prologue to *Pat Mulholland's Day*, the poetic "measure" (to use the old-fashioned term) is never obvious; nevertheless, it is there, part of the "magic." It is there, silently performing the function that Coleridge, Wordsworth, and Eliot among them say that poetic rhythm should perform: it is not only helping to express, by a kind of imitation, the emotion, the passion felt and to be conveyed; it is also controlling and containing it; it is alerting the hearer to the fact that this is not prose but something more important; and it is, by the rhythm of stressed syllables and echoed sounds in it, having the effect of a narcotic which lulls to sleep what is mundane and irrelevant in our minds so as to give greater freedom to what is relevant and vital.

Now, all traditional verse has two rhythms interacting on each other, the one fixed and regular (the meter, for example, iambic pentameter) and the other free (what is usually called the rhythm). In the kind of verse that Manson writes, another kind of rhythm takes the place of the fixed and formal meter of traditional verse, the beat of which is heard like a barely audible drum beat, as it were, underlying the free and flexible rhythmic movements of the second rhythm, which imitate what is being described or expressed. This underlying drum beat in Manson's kind of verse is not insistent, and it is not regular, but it is felt to be there. It is made up of assonances and alliterations and occasional rare rhymes and mid-rhymes (as rare as in *Lycidas,* for example), which make themselves heard like the louder throb of a distant drum. We have *zoom-loom-assume,* in the lines above, and elsewhere, *see-be, away-day, night-light, all-ball, sky-high, grey-day, green-seen, day-say.* Together these rare rhymes, the assonances, and the alliterations make up a subtle and rather irregular pattern, much more evident to the ear than to the eye—a pattern which underlies the imitative rhythm and is just sufficently formal to have the threefold effect—the "magic" which Wordsworth, Coleridge, and Eliot speak of, and which one feels so strongly in this Prologue.

Manson's language in the Prologue is very close to that of the dialogue in his play, for though only one man is speaking here, he is not soliloquizing but speaking directly to someone—to the audience. The difference between the language here and that of exchanges of speech between the dramatis personae is that their speech is very much affected by their characters and by the action, the mood, and the genre of each particular play.

The use of this kind of simple language, so like ordinary speech and yet not quite ordinary speech, and this kind of verse form, so like prose, and yet decidedly not prose, is one of the marks of Manson's originality, for it is his own spontaneous invention. I cannot think of any other playwright who uses verse like this— who has broken away from blank verse or the heroic couplet, neither of which seems to suit our modern speech rhythms, and writes natural dialogue which is nevertheless poetry—has all the effect of poetry, and yet does not create a barrier of strangeness between the play and its modern audience. This kind of thing is also a sign of his being a born dramatist. When two of Manson's plays were sent to that great and experienced actor, Sir Ralph Richardson, he commented on the beauty of the poetry and the fact that the writer had "a strong feeling for the theatre," and "a real understanding of dialogue." Mr. John Duncan Macrae, said to be the best actor on the Scottish stage, expressed a similar admiration for the poetic beauty of the language and the instinct for dialogue and "theatre."

These slight comments will serve, I hope, to hint to our readers, both overseas and at home, that London is not at present the place to look in for new and original dramatic writing—for drama which, though in no way derivative, yet belongs, as Dr. Leavis says the great American novels, such as those of Mark Twain and Nathaniel Hawthorne do, to the great tradition of English literature and drama. In the "swinging" London of today, the mass media seem to be making true originality and even artistic sanity impossible. But, judging by this one case (and South Africa has yielded other writers of merit), in the remoter and as yet not overpopulated regions of the English-speaking world, originality and sanity are still, though extremely rare, at least possible; and we hope in the rest of this book to do something toward justifying this thesis.

CHAPTER 2

Biography

I *Ancestry and Early Life*

A fostering childhood is perhaps partly what has enabled Manson to survive, as a writer, the frustrations of living in an age hostile to his most valuable qualities. In dealing very briefly with Manson's life, I shall leave out all reference to what is merely personal. A writer's personal life is strictly his own concern, and most of those who inquire into it are indulging, not in scholarship, as the world seems to believe, but in the questionable pleasures of gossip, or in amateur psychoanalysis at a disabling remove. I shall, therefore, apart from a few bare facts, speak only of his background, and tell one or two anecdotes illustrative of his inventiveness and dramatic bent.

Manson's ancestors were, on the father's side, partly Scandinavian but chiefly Scottish; on the mother's, Scandinavian. His grandfather was from the Shetland Islands and used to talk, he fully believed, to ghosts; the family all seem to have been born with strongly marked personalities. At the time of Manson's birth, his father, having fought in the 1914 war in the Southwest-African campaign, was settled on the African continent, where he had become an electrical engineer in the British Colonial Service in Tanganyika (now Tanzania). There Manson was born, January 29, 1926, in the little town of Tabora. He was the youngest of three children, Leonard, Audrey (called Winkey) and Harley (that is, H.W.D.).

In Tabora the family lived for nine years. Childhood in the Manson household must have been remarkably spacious, free, and adventurous, as childhood could be in the "outposts of empire" in those days, but it was not without discipline. The children were all fearless. "I think I did teach my children courage," says their mother. When the children fought, among themselves, and with the African and English boys, they fought wholeheartedly to win, observing no Queensberry rules. They hated a half-hearted approach to anything. Manson despised people who could not put their whole selves into work or games or fighting. He could be ruthless in his insistence on courage in everything: it is a universal duty, a virtue which it is shameful to lack. Though profoundly compassionate by nature, he had nevertheless no patience with "petty unselfishness," "coddled sensibilities," and "exaggerated solicitudes." *

The family members were all warmhearted, quick-tempered, and unconventional, with a passion for animals and all living things. And there were strange wild creatures where they lived. In Tabora they had a pet warthog, called Binty Marufu. Warthogs to most people are extraordinarily ugly: in the Mansons' animal-loving eyes, they are "charming." Binty Marufu used to sleep on the living-room sofa. Once, having crept under the kitchen stove for warmth, she arose in the morning with the stove on her back. And there were lions, even commoner then than now, and other beasts of prey in that world. Manson's mother, appreciating, like her children, the lion's point of view as well as her own, tells several stories about them. For example, one wet, stormy night, a missionary friend built a big fire in her living room. All at once, in the midst of buckets of rain, constant lightning, and crashing thunder, she heard a loud thumping on the front door. A wayfarer, come for refuge, she thought. She opened the door. Fortunately it opened inward, so that she remained behind it against the wall, for who should walk in but a huge black-maned lion, dripping wet and miserable! He had been lashing his tail against the door. The missionary froze, flattened against the wall; unaware of her, the lion appeared to welcome the blazing fire, for he walked straight to the hearth, shook himself all over like a big dog till he was nearly dry, then lay down on the hearthrug, stretched himself out, and soon, to the onlooker's huge relief fell fast asleep. Still as a mouse, she crept along the wall till she came to another door, quietly opened it, then locked it from the other side, locked all the inside doors, and warned the household. They spent a night of terror, until, at dawn, the storm having ceased, the lion woke up and walked off quietly home again.

On another dark night in Tanganyika several young men were

* The first phrase is from E. M. Forster, the other two from Henry James.

sitting in a bedroom, when they heard their host in the garden shouting in a high and startled voice, "What are *you* doing here! How dare you come into my garden! Get out at once! Get out!" and so on. He was addressing a leopard, and sheer fright had produced the indignant words. The leopard, too, was startled, for he made off without delay.

Those were the days, especially in the colonies, of many servants. Each of the children when small had his own particular African body servant, whose business it was to look after his special charge, often telling him wise and fascinating stories from African lore, and incidentally teaching him good manners and good morals, and checking and even punishing him when he behaved badly. The family all spoke Swahili, and there was mutual liking and respect. There was one man whose sole function it was to turn the handle of the old-fashioned gramophone, and there is a family photograph with him proudly holding up the gramophone handle, honorable symbol of his office. This kind of master-servant relationship is no bad thing, so long as it is not made too difficult for members of the servant class to rise to higher rank, even the highest. Certainly, on the average, relationships of this kind may make for more interesting and varied lives than many people realize, with stronger human interests on both sides of the line, each regarding the other's family as, in a way, his own, and genuinely participating in joys and sorrows that they would otherwise not share. In fact, a society of this kind may be good soil for the basic human virtues to grow in, and is a good nursery for the young creative mind. One cannot live as a child in wilder Africa, and grow up imagining that life and people are really as Wesker and Pinter and Beckett represent them.

II *Residence in England*

In 1933, the worst year of the great depression, the Manson family went to England on leave. Mr. Manson, like so many other colonial civil servants, was retrenched and, after nine months on pension, accepted a post in the Bahamas. There he remained, while Mrs. Manson took first a caravan and then a house in Ramsgate for the children. In the caravan they spent a pleasant year traveling all over England; the house was large and roomy, with a big garden, and the children were sent to school, Manson to Chatham House in Ramsgate. In this school his elder brother,

Leonard, and Edward Heath, four years Leonard's senior, acted together in one or two Aldwych farces.

Even in England the children lived a largely outdoor life, swimming in the sea, walking, cycling, climbing in the country, and scrambling about; they were wild creatures whom the polite English boys did not understand. They read voraciously, especially the future poet, in history, travel, war, biography, poetry, drama. Manson's memory was always remarkably retentive, which partly accounts for the astonishing quantity of general out-of-the-way knowledge which this man who disliked intensely the academic world and everything that smells of the lamp had accumulated.

In 1939 the Ramsgate house was sold, and at Christmas, three months after the outbreak of war, Mrs. Manson and the children moved to Johannesburg—except for Leonard, who had had a year's military training at Sandhurst, and had enlisted almost immediately. Manson was sent to school in the famous Saint Andrew's College in Grahamstown, South Africa. There he spent several tempestuous years, being beaten literally every day and, on one memorable day, when he had started off by meaning to be particularly good, no less than four times.

Manson's stories of his school days were full of the bright, tantalizing, satirical humor which often delighted even when it exasperated his victims. But even at that early age he possessed the poet's habit and gift of intently observing his fellows; his stories showed that he must have had a degree of compassionate insight most unusual in young boys. The insight had no doubt been deepened and enriched retrospectively—but tears were sometimes brought to the listener's eye by his tales of some school fellow or master, perhaps long dead—killed in the last war, most likely, for Saint Andrew's has always been a patriotic school, bound to ancestral Britain. One story concerns a school fellow in England, who, though able and clever, was so clumsy that he was physically almost an imbecile: he was always falling over his own feet, could not run, and was hopelessly bad at all sports. Manson, being especially strong, active, and nimble, was asked to take him in hand, and, by sheer patience and concentrated interest, he managed to teach him a modicum of physical skill. A few years later, however, this boy, then a man, was killed in World War II. One evening, not very many years ago, Manson was driving along not very far from Pietermaritzburg in the dusk. He was utterly exhausted and was in great danger of falling asleep at the wheel. Presently he became aware of his dead friend sitting beside him in the front of the car. The friend suggested that they should stop the car, get out, and go for a walk. This they did, walking and talking together in the gathering darkness. After awhile Manson found himself alone and refreshed. He went back to the car and continued the journey in safety. This story is not for the Psychical Research Society. The experience was produced, most likely, by the action upon a mind naturally creative of a number of things: a half-conscious sense of danger; an affectionate and intensely imaginative, though almost unconscious, memory of a personality; and a mind too exhausted to distinguish illusion from reality.

III *War Years*

After sitting for the matriculation exam at the end of 1943, Manson, then seventeen, without waiting for the results, enlisted; after training he was posted to the Natal Carbineers, with whom he served in Italy in 1944 and 1945.

Both Manson and his brother Leonard told enthralling and sometimes hair-raising stories from their inexhaustible store of tales about the 1939–45 war. From others and from each other one heard of their exceptional courage. Leonard, the elder by six years, won the Military Cross, but apart from that, was noted for always volunteering for the most dangerous jobs, like raiding a sleeping enemy camp in the small hours, with one or two companions, and bringing back a prisoner for interrogation. Since he too had a humane and imaginative nature, he told his younger brother that sometimes to that day when he thought of some exploit he had volunteered for, the cold sweat would break out on his forehead. Neither brother could understand how any young man could deliberately pass over the chance of war experience. Manson, though utterly free from the nonsense of "living dangerously" by indulging in perversion, drug-taking, and the like, yet never refused a personal challenge or avoided the need for manly action; certainly, the ultimate experiences of war bore fruit in the firsthand knowledge of life on which his plays are based.

IV *Further Education*

When the war was over, safely for both of them, the young men returned to their mother's flat in Johannesburg, at first in rather restless mood. (Both their mother and their sister Winkey had also contributed to the Allied war effort.) Leonard followed something of a family tradition by joining the British Colonial Service as an assistant commissioner; he later became a district commissioner and served in Nigeria, Tanganyika, and Bechuanaland, as they then were. But Manson decided to continue his education and enrolled at the University of the Witwatersrand, Johannesburg, where in due course he took a degree in English and fine art, for both of which he had exceptional talent. He had not only extremely unusual gifts as a writer but also had a strong leaning toward the plastic arts; as a child he used to love molding animals in clay; and to his last year he liked to draw with his fountain pen—delicate, lively line drawings of animals, full of movement and character, human figures, and lightning characterizations (not caricatures) of people. His first idea, he has said, was to be a painter, and the painter's habit of looking at everything carefully and with pleasure has entered very considerably into his writing.

I have in my possession to this day the fruit of a delightful invention of Manson's which illustrates both the talent for drawing and that for dramatic characterization. This fruit is a sheet of foolscap on which, apropos of someone nicknamed "Horse," he had begun by giving me an example of "Horse-writing," then "Crab-writing," "Fly-writing," "Moth-writing," etc., followed by a delicately executed line of each, each somehow a convincing expression of the kind of creature that was supposed to have written it. Presently this developed into a disquisition on Fish Poetry, with examples. (The examples are on the paper too.) There are, apparently, a special language and special rules of rhythm and rhyme for Fish Poetry. As it went on, the disquisition was being delivered by a particular individual of Manson's invention, a professor of insect graphology in Egypt, whose sideline was Fish Poetry—an extremely erudite character, an English gentleman from Oxford (not caricatured, but taken respectfully), very precise and with exquisite taste, but perhaps a little precious.

The ex-servicemen's university classes just after the war were most interesting to teach (I was lecturing at "Wits" at the time). One felt about the best of these men that they were not going to go meekly into any kind of job that offered them "security." They had known plenty of insecurity, and they had seen life and death; they were highly critical, and they had matured rapidly. They were men, and they had a strong sense of reality. When I first knew Manson there was still a certain deceptive softness about his features; with his bright gold hair, his bright blue eyes, and a remarkable look of physical power and liveliness about his whole rather stocky person, almost as if vitality were visibly streaming from him in rays, he reminded one of Perdita's phrase, "bright Phoebus in his strength." A year or two later he grew a bright gold beard, and this strengthened the impression.

The appearance of vitality, which he maintained throughout his life, did not belie him. He was the most inventive person most of his acquaintances had ever met. The family still tell a story of him as a little boy of ten or eleven, which is known as "The Canterbury Lie." One morning in Ramsgate he went off on his bicycle to play with a friend. He was to have been home by lunchtime, but the boys were enjoying themselves so much that when the friend's mother asked Harley to stay to lunch, he did so. In due course teatime came; after more hours of absorption, suppertime, and each time he yielded to the temptation to stay. At length it was bedtime, and he was persuaded to share his friend's bedroom. It was not till late the next day that he decided to cycle home to his distracted parents. They were quite mollified when the little boy told them that he had decided to go to look at Canterbury Cathedral and city and described everything that he had done and seen in the thirty-six hours—where he had spent the night, how he had got food and what he had eaten, all in minute and vivid detail. The family were delighted with his enterprise and originality in going so far and seeing so much all by himself at his tender age, and it was some days before the mine was exploded under him and the Canterbury lie blown to pieces.

V *Personality; Dramatic Inventiveness*

The Canterbury story illustrates his native gift for narrative and drama. It is illustrated even better by his practice when he went mountain climbing with his friend David Gillham (also an ex-

serviceman student with whom he shared a flat and a frugal bach-
elor existence in Johannesburg) of carrying on imaginary dialogues, in which there were two characters—God and a Johannesburg city slicker. God they called "the Oubaas" (a respectful and
affectionate term for an old Boer pater-familias and grandfather).
The Oubaas, of course, had created the world and was finally responsible for everything in it, but he was a little diffident because
the City Slicker had had a university education, and he had only
been trained at a technical college. He had a strong Afrikaans
accent. When there was a particularly gorgeous sunset, the City
Slicker (both young men took part in the dialogue) would com-
plain that it was rather vulgar and overdone; the Oubaas, feeling
a little ashamed of his unsophisticated taste, would nevertheless
stoutly maintain that, for his part, he liked it. When the Slicker
complained about something in the world that the Oubaas really
should have managed better, the Oubaas would explain that he
had been sick or absent that day and that an apprentice had
botched the job.

Some years later when a famous character entered Manson's
life, a similar kind of dialogue would take place continually between him and Manson and Manson's first wife, or any friend who
happened to be present. This character was his beloved dachs-
hund, Dunkel, a quite outstandingly intelligent and charming
creature of decided and most dignified personality, who lived to a
reverend old age and died more deeply and sincerely mourned
than many human beings ever are or deserve to be. But it is hard
for Manson's friends to distinguish with absolute certainty between what Dunkel really was and the character Manson, by
these dialogues and the marvelous tales he told about Dunkel's
exploits, constantly built up around him. Moreover, as the great
zoologist, Konrad Z. Lorenz, would agree, the way he was treated
greatly developed his intelligence and responsiveness and increased his native gentlemanliness and distinction.

After a rich and varied past, during which, among other things,
according to Manson, he had won the Iron Cross in World War I,
and inspired most of the great works of painting, music, and literature in the world, Dunkel was flown secretly by some of his ad-
mirers in the Luftwaffe to Johannesburg. There he looked around
for a suitable slave (the dogs are the masters of the world, human
beings their slaves, whose first duty it is to provide them with

food, shelter, and proper comforts); he fixed upon Manson, trotted into his house one morning, and enslaved him for ever. "Beware! Beware!" Manson used to quote: "His flashing eyes, his floating hair!" * He used to accompany Manson on all car journeys, sitting on the back seat with a paw on his friend's shoulder, his eyes eagerly spying out objects of interest, his voice aggressively raised against any traditional enemy along the roadside; and once or twice, as to the manner born, he rode with him on his motorbike, for he had the princely accomplishment of making himself quite at home, with all his usual dignity, in any circumstances. Among the works which he inspired by sitting quietly, or even sleeping, beside the reputed author were Manson's plays, and whenever any critical friend accused him of having written for any of his authors a faulty passage or a bad tale he would merely say "Wa-all!" and leave it at that.

Dunkel was a wise and spirited dog with a most sensitive and loving nature, who bore his sufferings in old age with reserve and stoicism, still enjoying life as much as he could. Yet the Dunkel Manson's friends knew was partly created, as a character in a play is created, by the enduring "illusion" thrown over him by the words of his master—an illusion as convincing as that which Athene threw over Ulysses when he first returned to Ithaca. And the personality inside the illusion was a character full not only of the animal virtues which human guilt makes it impossible for people to possess, but of the near-human ones which the imaginative appreciation and deep affection with which he was surrounded had helped to develop to the utmost degree possible to an animal.

I could give scores more examples of the fertility of Manson's dramatic imagination, often shot through with entertaining fantasy. It is essentially a dramatic imagination, expressing itself in his everyday conversation in impromptu dialogue, character, and even plot. Like his brother Leonard, who has set several of Shakespeare's songs to music, he had a fine ear and was an excellent mimic. In giving a political or social opinion, he became in a flash, now Mr. Wilson, now Mr. Smith, now Mr. Vorster, now a typical follower of any of them, a British Tory, a pop star, a dock worker, and so on—and, incidentally, though he had strong opinions they

* From Coleridge's *Kubla Khan.*

were never quite party ones. I give two examples of this impromptu gift:

Once, as several friends were having, first, supper in a café, and then walking down to a bioscope (movie) in Johannesburg to see a Danny Kaye picture (they all delighted in the brilliant Danny Kaye of those days) Manson became, as they talked and walked, three people in a YMCA hostel, each speaking with his own voice and accent—a very decent young German, bitterly ashamed of the Nazis (this was in the early 1950's) and trying, rather clumsily, to defend himself; a sardonic, clever Frenchman who, with an apt French phrase and a cruel wit, defeated and turned the German's words against himself every time; and an Italian with a roving eye, who was not much interested in the conversation. The friends were so much enthralled by the story as it unrolled that they changed their plans to see the Danny Kaye movie and went into another café instead.

And once, in Cape Town, over afternoon tea in Cecil Higgs's (the painter's) flat, Manson began to be a couple of New Zealanders having a discussion about the son of one of them. The father feared that the son might have a "yellow streak." (The reason why took an entertaining half-hour or so to emerge, but it turned out in the end that this was because he wanted to be a painter and preferred painting to football.) As the story developed, two more characters entered the room, the wives of the two men, one of them summoned from across the fence by her husband, the other from the kitchen, and, as far as I remember, a boy or two. We were happily entertained all through a summer's afternoon by this story, and by the persons summoned up, all in New Zealand accents, and in a spirit very sympathetic toward New Zealanders in general.

Every anecdote retold here reflects the dramatic form which Manson's inventiveness quite naturally assumed, in extempore dialogue or plot, for he was a born dramatist as well as a born poet. My retelling does not, alas, recapture the sparkle and gaiety with which the stories were told. More important, it does not give any idea of the powerful impression which his personality made on all who knew him. He was a man of charm, but he was also formidable, a man to be afraid of, and a friend to be trusted absolutely. This was because of his ruthless, rockbottom honesty, his fearlessness, and a most passionate concern for quality. Only on such virtues could writing of the stature of H. W. D. Mason's be built.

Manson's death, at the early age of forty-three, on May 29, 1969, came as a stunning shock to all who knew him. At three o'clock on a sunny afternoon he was riding gaily down a quiet country road on his motorbike to post a letter when a collision, unwitnessed and unexplained, occurred between him and a ten-ton lorry. I have never seen so many grown men weep, Africans and whites alike, as on that day. Everybody found it almost impossible to believe that a man so exceptionally strong and sturdy, so charged with vitality, and of so rich and striking a personality, could in a flash cease to be. He left behind him his wife and a fifteen-month-old daughter.

CHAPTER 3

Unposted Letter

BEFORE going on to discuss the plays I should like to quote
in full, and give some analysis of, one of Manson's rare poems
—the one called *Unposted Letter,* and published in *Theoria.*
There are few of these, because Manson usually needs the scope
offered by full-scale drama.

I've written and told you before about it, Jack,
But it's true.
One good green day, I feel, is all I need.
One good green day.
It's green enough today you'd say if you were here.
But that's not true.
It's nothing like green enough.
That's what I'd like to explain to you.
The thick, rich, green kikuyu grass is long,
Still spikey, standing up like spears,
Not all yet tumbled down and looping,
Not yet sending out suckers and winding round everything that
     grows,
Or beginning to climb the trees and fences.
But it's growing. Everything is growing—too fast for me.
I feel in a way left behind by it all.

I have lemon trees, you know, to look at.
I have honey-suckle (in flower) growing
On a rickety arch of wire that Uncle Arthur's made
Just over the gate
And it smells most sweetly at dusk,
And in the early morning too,
I have geraniums (climbers) pink ones,
A few frail flowers here and there, but mostly leaf
Growing up against the fence.
And the leaves of geraniums, this sort anyway,
With the small pink flowers,

Are so green on a still, moist morning like this
You feel a sort of frenzy rising up inside you
Just looking at them—
As if you were a painter or something—
And had sat there, as I have often, just looking
And thinking of *how* to show it—
How to make men see
How all of it glows so and grows
Into—what?—that seems to matter so?
But maybe if you could make men see
Just how much sunlight green has trapped inside it
That people cannot see,
You'd be able to answer Uncle Arthur
When he keeps asking what I'm looking at.
He's anxious, I suppose, and thinks I'm only brooding.
And I have been brooding—but not about what he thinks.
And you mustn't misunderstand me either.
One good green day inside is all I need
And something will stir.
Everything—as you predicted—has been—
How can I say it—well, both ridiculous and sad somehow.
All smiles—a bit too near to tears.
And it's unnerved me.
You see, when they called for me at the station
(Just Uncle Arthur and Aunt Janey)
They brought the half-ton.
'For all my goods and chattels', they said—meaning the wheel
        chair.
And they loaded it up on the back
And tied it down with bits of rope
But the damned thing rolled and slammed about
Like a thing possessed
Round every curve we took up Town Hill—all the way up.
We didn't stop for the view on top like we used to.

But nothing's changed, not a single thing, except what's natural
        and seasonal,
Some wattle stripped and lying bare—
And further on some mealies there where lucerne seemed
Perhaps what you expected as the truck swung round some curve.
But at the turn-off there was something new . . .
I'm not sure whether I like it.
A real, stone, cut-stone, shelter for the milk cans
With a neat, new, yellow thatch on it like a proper little cottage—

And somehow silly.
But it will last for years,
And, as Aunt Janey says, it really does keep the milk cans cool.

And then there was the arrival—
And what seemed like a hundred black and helping hands—
And the damned wheel chair—all shiny—new—standing there
    unloaded.
They lowered me into it most solemnly.
We were all a bit shaky when we finally got inside.
But it was dim and cool inside as always.
The granadilla (growing thick now, full of green, young fruit)
Let what light we needed through
To look as much as we dared to at each other.
They'd cut enough of it back, I could see,
To allow me a view of the river,
And it had been freshly done—that morning probably—
Before they came for me.

After tea Uncle Arthur went outside 'to attend to things',
And that left Aunt Janey and me alone in the room.
It wasn't as bad as all that either. It really wasn't.
Almost jolly. And supper was too.
And then bed.
That was the worst bit.
You see, they didn't want to help me,
But couldn't for the life of them imagine how I managed it.
And, of course, I couldn't manage completely. I undressed though,

And shouted for them.
And they were both there—at the door—a bit too quickly.
Such agony of thwarted love in both their eyes,
Such doubts as how to do what they had to do without offending
    me
That I didn't know whether to laugh or cry.
But there wasn't any need to pretend anything.
I'd forgotten how strong the old man was—
How easily we've seen him, many times, heave—no, throw—
A sack of mealies bang up against the back of the truck.
And that's how he handled me.
One—two—three! And up into bed. No trouble at all.
And Aunt Janey kissed me—just once—softly,
And he did too—
The same old tobaccoey, bristly kiss.

You don't exactly stretch out when you have nothing to stretch
        out—
It's something like it—but a briefer thing—
And I'd just snuffed out the candle, grateful for the dark,
And was doing just that,
When I heard him at the door again.
"What's it?" I asked. The door opened. I could see him dimly.
"Boy?"
"Yes" I said.
"What do you do if you want a pee?"
"I can manage."
He didn't go away. He didn't see how,
"How?"
It wasn't curiosity. He just didn't believe me. And I was angry.
"I've got a bloody bottle!" I shouted.
"D'you want to see it?"
"Oh. I see." He paused for a second . . . "A bottle . . . I'm
        sorry."
And he closed the door.

Three weeks later—
I didn't post this letter, I'm afraid,
But you needn't worry. I'm quite O.K.
You don't think so, do you?
And now you're going to worry too—like them. Well, don't.
You just worry about getting back, see? In one piece.
And I don't mean that quite either.
I'm in one piece. If a bit abbreviated.
And that remark will worry you too—I know you.
Well, what am I to do?
You can't lie down and cry, can you?
And the sky's been weeping. Not one sunny day—
Not one that lasted anyway—since I last wrote.
Just one green day I wanted. What was I hoping for?
You just come back, see?
That'll be a green enough day for me.

And let's not stick about here, hey? Promise?
Pile me in the front seat with you
And let's ride—fast—wherever you like—
Any place that's to hell out of here.
Up through the Dargle, high up over Balgowan if you like.
And wherever we like, we'll stop, shall we?
At any old pub.

And we'll come singing home.
That'll be a green day for me.
You just come back, that's all.

P.S. And what's the use of posting this to you—now?
And how would I address it?
Care of some dark hole in the ground?
Forgive that last, most desperate quip of all,
Old mole, my brother.
Burrow however deep down into the dark
And I will hear you.
Make sounds as slight as mice feet skittering
And I shall hear.
I shall hear
If you make sounds like a rose unfurling
Or falling snow.
Lie as still as a stone through summer or winter,
Whiten away to a bare bone,
And I will hear you.
You will be as green as any tree to me, my brother, for ever
Though these ruled leaves go yellow and rot.
Our *life* together will be
All the green days I shall ever ask for—God forgive me!

I think everybody will admit in the first place that this poem is
extremely moving, and in the second, that the way in which the
story is told seems completely natural. The feeling in it is absolutely genuine, felt by the author at the greatest possible depth,
and communicated entirely without tricks, though with considerable art. To communicate feeling, no matter how genuine, however, is not the whole of the serious writer's intention: he aims at
communicating, in moving the reader, also something of the
meaning, the value of life. For, as W. B. Yeats says in writing of
Wilfred Owen, passive suffering is not a fit subject for poetry.
Though a sense of the meaning and the value of the various and
often harrowing emotions communicated in *Unposted Letter* does
pervade the entire poem, that sense is not crystallized until we
reach the postscript, and then suddenly there it lies alive and shining like a precious jewel at the bottom of a glass of water. The
effect there is one of purest poetry.

In this respect, *Unposted Letter* (which is virtually a dramatic
monologue) is typical of Manson's own peculiar type of dramatic

verse. It goes along, sounding like ordinary natural speech, though it is never quite prose, until suddenly, at moments of specially concentrated emotion, as here in the postscript, it bursts into flame, as it were, leaps up in a pure blaze of passion, and illuminates with its intense and lovely light everything that has gone before. The story is allowed to act itself out, as a story should. When the young soldier who has had both his legs blown off describes his homecoming, where the misery of all concerned is sternly controlled, it is all "well, both ridiculous and sad somehow." Home, we gather, is the Natal farm on which the protagonist and his brother have, as orphans, been brought up by their "Uncle Arthur and Aunt Janey." To those who know the terrain, the farm is near Pietermaritzburg: it is unmistakably in South Africa, recognizably in Natal.

The affection between the brothers is felt in the candor with which the letter writer who, one gathers, is normally in his youngmanly way, rather proud and reserved, refers to his helpless plight and the painful embarrassment with which it fills the three deeply moved white people at their railway station meeting for the first time after the calamity. The young man's relationship with the old couple is subtly indicated, and the profundity and delicacy of their affection for him are felt in many details such as their talking of his "goods and chattels" when they mean his wheelchair, or their trying so desperately hard not to do anything for him unless it is strictly necessary. This respect for the manhood of the child they once looked after, now that the war has robbed him forever of his manly independence, shows how sensitive sheer affection and compassion have made them, and we are made to realize the beauty of their behavior, even though it might have been easier for him to be treated more crudely. There is a delicacy too in "the black and helping hands" of the Zulu farm hands, some of whom may be strangers to him.

The same imaginative delicacy in the old couple is shown in the way they have had the granadilla creeper freshly cut away—"that morning probably"—so that he can see the view of the river from where he will have to sit, for such long hours, day after day, at the living-room window. The account of his going to bed is almost unbearably moving: every detail makes the reader feel, with piercing reality, as if he were there, almost as if he were they, the agonizing strain for all three of the characters; he feels also a deep respect for the old couple, especially Uncle Arthur when he persists in his inquiry about the urine bottle.

But, we are made to feel, good as Uncle Arthur and Aunt Janey are to him, fond as he is of them, the invalided soldier is young; he is active by nature and habit, and the bottled-up energy and the cruelly frustrated adventurousness in him soon become almost too much to bear. He longs to get out and away. In the part of the letter written "three weeks later," Manson makes us feel, in the short, restless sentences of his third to last verse (the letter writer has no heart now for giving detailed impressions of anything) that the restlessness has become too urgent, the young man has fixed his desires too desperately on his brother's return from the war, and he is suddenly terrified, the words suggest, lest his brother should be hurt or killed before he can come back. A depth of longing for his brother and his brother's young male companionship sounds in the lines that end: "You just come back, see? That'll be a green enough day for me."

The strength of feelings that are seldom openly and never fully expressed seems to make those last two lines quiver with the attempt at control, and the same quality is felt in the slight self-consciousness of the next ten lines—in them one is made to feel in every part the shyness of a young man, trained as young men are at school and at home not to be "sentimental," never to express affection or mental suffering, conflicting with the passionate need to see his brother again. Both emotions are mingled with the urge to get out and away from the house and the company to which he is confined—to feel free, to be a young man again on equal terms with another young man, to get drunk, and to drive about fast in the open air.

All this has been poignantly conveyed, and in it all the reader feels and sympathizes with the slight degree of very natural self-pity that runs through the words, and especially with the letter writer's longing for his brother's company. The tie between those who were once children together in the same family, has, as Jane Austen says, "aspects in which even the conjugal tie is beneath the fraternal." The speaker's helpless condition, the parting between the brothers, and the dangers of war, have, moreover, sharply intensified his longing for a reunion. Now, we learn from the postscript, it is not to be. His brother has been killed, and the speaker has vastly more reason than ever to pity himself.

But in the last verse of all every trace of self-pity and every trace of self-consciousness have been swept right out of the young man's mind by the rush, the flood of a greater grief than he has ever yet known. No one is going to read his letter now, his brother is not going to be embarrassed by it, and the depth of his affection may now be freely felt and expressed in it.

For the first moment he is bitter: "P.S. And what's the use of posting this to you—now?/And how would I address it?/Care of some dark hole in the ground?" His brother has had even worse luck than he has, for he is dead. He is even worse confined than the writer—not in a pleasant, familiar home, open to sun and light and air, and looked after by devoted friends, but shut up in some dark hole in the ground, cold and alone for ever. As the writer's own words bring this home to him, the reality expels his own troubles from his mind and fills him with remorse: "Forgive that last, most desperate quip of all,/Old mole, my brother." He thinks of Hamlet's words and feels, with Hamlet, the dreadful sadness of death, of the dead man's having become, as it were, a blind, burrowing mole forever in the underground darkness and dampness and confinement of the grave. But we are made to realize that this awful sadness and the intensity of his forever-to-be-frustrated longing for his brother mean that he understands his unique value; and this understanding is the precious jewel that the toad, so ugly and venomous, wears in its head. He will have to give up for ever even the slightest desperate hope of ever hearing his brother again even by as much of a sound as is made by a rose unfurling or a snowflake falling. (How intensely those comparisons make one feel the extremity of his loss.) And yet he will always be intensely aware of him; the fact that his brother *has been* and that he has known him so intimately is enough: he is ashamed of having asked for more. It is a value as green as the light in a geranium leaf.

I shall not discuss such matters as the verse form, the dramatic method, the solid creation of character and environment by means of all kinds of subtle and many-faceted detail—the kikuyu grass, the shelter for milk cans, for example, the good-night kisses, and finally the passage about the geranium leaves. The young man is a quite well-educated country boy, neither a poet nor a philosopher, but he is keenly aware of an indefinable something that he cannot quite crystallize or express—some kind of central value—an illuminating beauty at the heart of all life: in a way it is as much in a geranium leaf as in anything else. He stumbles at an expression of it, and what he ventures in the lines suggesting how worried Uncle Arthur is about his listlessness, and ending, "One good green day inside is all I need/And something will stir" makes us understand what he means by "green."

And something does stir most powerfully. The "good green day" does not come joyfully, as he had hoped it would, with the return of his brother. It comes with possibly the greatest grief he will ever know—with his brother's death. The greenness that comes lies in the full and clear understanding of what his brother has meant and always will mean to him. Hidden in that black well of grief is something that we might call joy: "Our *life* together will be/All the green days I shall ever ask for—God forgive me!"

CHAPTER 4

The Green Knight

MANSON'S first play, *The Fight at Finnsburgh*, begun in his student days at the University of the Witwatersrand, has never been published or produced because its length makes it (though full of beauties) unsuitable for performance. Like Chaucer's *Troilus & Criseyde* or Richardson's *Clarissa* it *needs* unusual length to convey the effect of the wear and tear of time on the main characters. It is now to be published as it stands, as a dramatic poem, by the University of the Witwatersrand Press, Johannesburg.

I *The Play and Its Source*

His second play, *The Green Knight*, the latest of all to be published so far, was the first to be performed. I myself and a colleague produced it with an almost completely student cast in Pietermaritzburg in 1955. The actor-students thoroughly enjoyed every aspect of the play—they found it eminently actable, and their delight in its quality was warmly expressed—"Isn't it wonderful," they would say at rehearsals, "to think that there is someone alive today who can write like this." Alan Paton's son Jonathan played the youthful but manly part of Gawain; the audience was enthusiastic, and the author received an ovation. The play combines dramatic excitement and humor with strong and deep feeling, and there is a fusion of delicacy and strength in the language and rhythm that gives the romantic story a fresh and new beauty, something real and individual. For the poetry is not an "embellishment"; it is the very breath and life of a truly dramatic play.

The story is founded on the anonymous Middle English poem, *Sir Gawain and the Green Knight,* a famous and most beautiful, vigorous, and lively poem. As Manson explains in the Postscript, the impulse to write this play was given him by an interpretative essay on the ancient poem by John Speirs in *Scrutiny*. The play is very far from being a mere dramatization of the poem.

In both medieval poem and modern play the main purpose is to show how, when a civilization has begun to decay, the individuals in it must, in order to escape the deathly infection of its falseness and corruption, have recourse to some central and natural power of life within themselves. In both, the beginnings of decay are to be found in Arthur and his Round Table of Knights. In both this force of life from which men should draw is symbolized by the Green Knight; in both the challenge he represents is accepted by Sir Gawain; and in both the Green Knight, under his alias of Sir Bercilak, by persuading his own wife to try to seduce him, tempts Gawain to break his Round Table vow of chastity. But in the medieval poem, Sir Gawain, with the most admirable grace and courtesy, resists the lady, except that he kisses her and accepts a gift from her. In the play the temptation has a very different purpose: Bercilak tempts both Gawain and his own wife because he wants them to choose what is real and living for themselves. Therefore in the play Gawain not only kisses and accepts from Enid the marriage gift given her by her husband, the Green Girdle; he sleeps with her too, and eventually they go off together with the Green Knight's blessing.

The idea behind this, it is clear from the poetry, is that the real and natural bond of passion, of the strong, natural, instinctual feeling of one human being for another—a passion including lust, but stronger, deeper, and much more lasting—must transcend a mere vow, based on theory, and now meaningless to both Gawain, who had sworn it, and Enid who had professed to admire it. The lady's marriage is a not-quite-human thing, her husband being a god: he cannot suffer because of her loving another man. In the play, a further complexity is deliberately given to the moral by Sir Gawain's having, before ever he started on his quest, won and returned the love of a young girl, Rosamund. This fact slightly qualifies the happy ending for Gawain, making it less unrealistic than it otherwise would be, for, as the last chorus suggests, though in the search for a real and enduring relationship between a man and a woman, vows must sometimes in the course of nature be broken and loyalties change, this can seldom happen without suffering for the deserted, and reflected suffering for the deserter.

II *Opening Scenes*

The Green Knight begins with a chorus of three voices. The
Green Knight being a force of nature, a strong sense of the changing seasons runs through both medieval poem and modern play.
The five choruses in the play all emphasize change—change of
seasons (the action takes a full year) but also the natural changes
in individual lives and in civilizations, which can be as wholesome
as the change of seasons.

The first act, an exciting one, takes place at Arthur's court at
Camelot on New Year's Eve. There is a feeling of excitement in
the words of the opening chorus, as they stand before the closed
curtain. The chorus, too, is listening intently for the play to begin,
and as it describes the approach of the actors, who are still unseen, we feel that something important is going to happen. The
noises off-stage—snatches of carol-singing and laughter in the distance—add to this. I should like to quote the whole, but can give
only a fragment:

First Voice.   Christmas has come—and gone.
              And tonight is New Year's Eve.
(*Again, very faintly in the distance, the noise of carol-singing and
laughter is heard and fades away.*)

Third Voice.   Now on platter and on gilded goblet, in the still
               red wine,
               Over the roof and on every rafter
               Flickers the firelight in the empty hall.

Second Voice.   Outside, heard if a window is thrown open,
               Or on the stone-cold balconies, is the sound of the
               river
               Slipping past the shallow cress banks,
               Clattering coldly the loose flat stones of the ford.

First Voice.   Beyond, across the white fields,
               Palely through the mist that lifts along the river
               banks,
               Through the fuzzy brush of the leafless forest,
               Glim dim and faint the lights of Camelot
               On New Year's Eve.

All the thousands of pounds spent on decor, landscape effects, and the huge cast of "supers" in costly clothes in the recent film musical, *Camelot*, do not give one-tenth as vivid an impression as these few lines do of the beauty of the wintry landscape without and the festive scene within. How comfortable and happy a sense of indoor warmth and gaiety, combined with a certain simple and bare but royal splendor, is given by the twenty-five little words of the first verse! And in the next two verses, giving, first, the sound of the wintry river nearby as heard from the castle windows or balconies (and through it a visual impression), and then (the words making something as exact, in such details, for example, as "fuzzy brush" or "glim, dim and faint," as a piece of Breughel painting), the further view of the faint sparse lights of the town with the forest undergrowth and naked trees between. As in a Shakespeare play, the poetry paints the scenery better than most scene painters could. And the beat of the rhythm is exciting, with its assonances and its almost regular pattern of alliteration strongly emphasized, almost as in the Middle English source poem. As the chorus goes on after the following stage directions:

(*The sound of processional music and many people talking together can be heard off-stage.*
There is an increase in the noise behind the curtain.)
The King is in the hall!

Presently with a fanfare the curtain opens to reveal the Great Hall, with festive table set, and the procession moves in, laughing and chattering.

By these very simple means the audience has been quieted, their minds have been made responsive to the crystal-clear, youthful kind of poetry, with a sort of romantic, fairy-tale aura about it, that is to come, and an eager curiosity about what is going to happen to the King and his court in this hall has been excited. It is, in fact, one of the best play-openings I know.

The play has romantic, fairy-tale aura, with a sort of lightness and gaiety. It is a love story with a good deal of suspense and a happy ending. And yet, at the core it is completely real, utterly sincere, and outspoken. It takes love and courage and life and death with a thorough seriousness that gives the whole play a singularly candid beauty, a quality of innocence and purity.

The play uses various devices to avoid the tedium and prolixity of realism. For example, in this first act, the exposition is done quickly and interestingly by making the jester's mental comments on the court, as he sits there in a fit of silent abstraction, audible to us, while the conversation and laughter of the rest of those round the dining table are unheard. A suddenly audible laugh rouses him. The King observes and speaks to him; the talk and laughter are loud again—and the complication begins.

It becomes clear from the jester's unhappy comments and his way of sailing too near the wind with one character after another that Guenivere and Lancelot are lovers, that Arthur knows it and suffers, but respects their genuine feeling, that the Round Table ideal of chastity has been broken by many, that corruption is spreading, and that Gawain, a young knight newly come from Yorkshire, sees it, grieves for his hero, Arthur, and disapproves of the rest. The jester's innuendos soon go too near the bone for Arthur. Suffocated by the sudden realization of the corruption, all at once Arthur calls for the door to be opened and the winter let in.

III   *Entry of the Green Knight*

Then comes a tremendous moment. Suddenly the door is blown open to the sound of a colossal wind, and the Green Knight strides in. His appearance is startling, and the onlookers gasp with horror. He is seven feet tall, with long green hair and beard, and he is dressed from head to foot in green.

He strides into the room and addresses the terrified group while the priest incoherently babbles prayers. His voice is loud, strong, and hearty, with a discernible north-country accent. Where is the "Governor of this gang?" he calls. Arthur pulls himself together and welcomes him courteously and with dignity, asking his name. "My name! Ha! Ha! Ha! Do I need a *name?*" cries the Green Knight, and, drawing attention in vivid verse to his green locks, like river weeds, green face, stature tall as a tree, and eyelashes like grass, he ends, "I'm the Green Man, What other name would fit me?" And when Arthur, his voice almost trembling, asks where he comes from, he gives an equally vivid account of the vast and frozen North from which he comes. His speech gives in every phrase, first, an intensely brilliant idea of the Green Knight's appearance, and of the fusion of beauty and horror in it, powerfully suggesting that he is a natural force and that nature can be both lovely and terrifying; then, of a region far beyond human ken, though with resemblances to the earth. Everything in it suggests that the Knight is both natural and supernatural—that force of life in nature which comes from something beyond the nature we know. There is clearly something cruelly hard and exacting as well as lovely in this force. He has come to see, he explains, "Who will play the Green Knight's game?" Will Arthur or any of his knights dare to pick up his enormous ax and strike off his head, on one condition:

> Don't be afeared, *I* shall bear the first blow,
> As bare as a baby's bottom.
> Let any lad latch on to this.   Who'll catch any axe
> And cut my neck-bone clean?   What offers?
> Come on!
> I shall pay him back with my blow
> This day a year from now.
> Who'll play football with my head?

There is a mixture of huge and terrible energy, mocking robust humor, and scorn of weakness in the vivid alliterative, strongly but irregularly rhythmic language (so like, when the Green Knight is there, the verse of Middle English). The combination of comedy, vigor, and poetry in the role is irresistible.

Even Arthur is more than a little taken aback. When Gawain sees this, he asks leave to volunteer for the job. After a good deal of cheerful mockery, the Green Knight carefully arranges a cushion on the floor, kneels, and bends down with his head conveniently placed for being chopped off. Gawain, after a shudder, deals him a tremendous blow with the huge ax, and the head comes rolling off. The court shrieks with horror. Not perturbed, the Green Knight gets up headless and picks up the severed head. "Hold my head a moment," he cries, throwing it to Gawain, who involuntarily catches it. "Don't drop it" cries the Green Knight; Gawain, half hysterical, begs him to take it back. "You see, I'm indestructible," says the Green Knight, doing so.

It is an exciting and comical scene, though with an undertone of mystery, and it ends with the Green Knight's making an appointment with Gawain to meet him in a year's time to have the blow

returned. "Ask for the Green Chapel," he says. "Travel North, and
you'll find me, never fear." He starts to go, then suddenly turns:
"Oh, I forgot!—my head!" (*He picks up his head by the hair and
stalks out of the open door. As he leaves a hurricane of wind is
heard and a chorus of wolf howls, then the galloping sound of a
huge horse, which is drowned in a bellow of terrific laughter.*)

IV *Gawain's Renunciation and Pilgrimage*

The second act opens with a chorus describing how more than
half the year has passed in delightful Camelot since New Year's
Eve. There is great charm in the verses about spring and summer,
with a dreamy, contented music in the vivid but economical picture given of happy life in Camelot. Then come ominous verses,
full of a deepening threat, suggesting decay and death as autumn
changes to winter, with "dead stick, old weed, sheep corpse" on
the now swollen and turbulent river.

The curtains part to show where on the river bank "Gawain and
his squire stand red-cheeked, their cloaks blustered by the wind"
(they sound like little more than boys) and the squire tries in vain
to persuade Gawain against the quest, which is bound to end in
death at the Green Knight's hands. At this point Rosamund enters,
and a short but skillful and touching scene follows. The young
Northern knight, at the thought of death, is suddenly overcome
with desire, and he roughly demands that she shall give herself to
him—"here, / Now, in the long grass by the river bank." Rosamund is reluctant. But, the poetry subtly indicates, when she sees
his eyes darkened, his forehead sweating, and realizes the terrible
sincerity and desperate urgency of Gawain's passion, she softens.
Feeling this, his violence turns to gentleness, and because her
hands are cold, Gawain will not accept what he feels to be a sacrifice (though she loves him), and he sends her gently back to the
palace.

Act III, which contains four scenes, is in many ways the best act
in the play. A chorus tersely gives an intense idea of the miseries
of Gawain's dogged and frozen, desperate, and seemingly endless
progress northward. When the scene opens in Bercilak's castle of
Haut Desert a year after Act I, just after Christmas, we gather
from the talk of servants that Gawain has arrived there nearly
dead and half crazy from exhaustion and exposure, and is now
upstairs ill in bed. The ladies of the castle—Lady Thora, Ber-

cilak's mother; Lady Enid, his wife; and his cousin, Lady Una—are eagerly discussing the guest, of whose feat of cutting off the Green Knight's head they have heard, with some skepticism, vague rumors. From very slight touches we deduce that these Northern ladies are all three very different from those of Arthur's court, more unsophisticated, hardier, and used to far fewer gaieties and distractions.

As they are discussing the Green Knight, in whose existence Lady Thora devoutly believes, Sir Bercilak enters silently and stands listening. At this point the strange, rather terrifying magical element that was present in Act I makes itself powerfully but subtly felt, and we become aware by degrees that Bercilak *is* the Green Knight, unknown to his wife and mother or to anyone else. He speaks, for example, with a North-country accent like the Green Knight's, which becomes more and more pronounced in his mockery; and his laugh resembles that of the Green Knight in Act I. His identity has been already hinted at by the chorus when they describe Gawain's journey and the tales told of

> —huge, strange spoors in the snow,
> —Only Bercilak of Haut Desert,
> Was mad enough in the head to know
> Of things that grow as tall as a tree.

This reminds us of the Green Knight's words: "I am green—as a tree—hair hands and face, / Tall as a tree."

Now, as the ladies talk of the Green Knight, we are made aware of an eerie coldness passing through the room on the stage for a moment, and over the audience. Bercilak's mother feels it most. "Is it true he's here looking for the Green Knight?" asks Una about Gawain, and Enid comments, in language of which the words and rhythm suggest that her flesh creeps at the weirdness of what she suspects:

> What a thing to have on your mind when you are sick
> and frozen.
> Last week George, the charcoal burner,
> Came across a body in the forest,
> Torn and bloody in the snow.
> No one knows who it was—
> There were foot marks all about it, round ones, weird,

> Not animal or human.
> He says it was the Green Knight again.

Bercilak. Wolves!

Enid.   (*almost shrieking*). Oh . . . Oh, God!

This is a very dramatic moment, rather ghostly, yet comical, strongly hinting at Bercilak's true identity. The women insist that the Green Man really does haunt the forest and has often been seen there. By this time their words make us devoutly believe it:

Lady Thora. The legend goes he's all green,
          And rides alone on a huge green horse
          Where the forest is thickest and the wind so still
          That not a twig-shiver or rabbit-scurry unsettles the snow
          Or snaps the frozen silence.
          The saplings bend back a path for him,
          The soft snow stiffens under his horse,
          The rivers make him ice bridges that he may cross them,
          Neither thicket, snowdrift nor swirling river
          Impedes his progress.

A vivid sense of supernatural powers and an uncanny sense of a supernatural presence are evoked by these lines. And at the same time the pure, clear, unaffected poetry, with a natural strength in its flexible texture, gives an indelible impression of the lonely depths of a forest deep in midwinter snow. Bercilak mocks at the womenfolk:

Bercilak. You're as superstitious as a pair of old woodcutters
          Caught out in the creaking night when the wolf-packs hunt
          And the whickering wind or the uncanny light of the shifting moon,
          Flickers twig shadows on the forest floor,
          And sets their hair on end.
          What will they make of the movement of shadows?
          What will they see at the moment the moon fades?
          Any rider in the forest is the Green Knight then.

Enid.	You can brush it aside: I've heard and seen too much.
	Once when you were out at night
	And the thin branch-shadows were waving their arms
	around and in our room,
	I heard the sound of something singing
	Like a cold breath carrying sound that spoke
	Over the frozen tops of the pine trees.
Thora.	Oh, God. Why do we pretend? I've heard it myself—
	The same cold breathy song.
Enid.	When the thing sings it seems to me as if the moon
	becomes unbearably bright,
	Till the snow flares with a stark white light.
Thora.	Once I saw in the whiteness
	A huge horse and a great green man leading it,
	Behind them three wolves walked
	As tame as dogs.

There is something appalling and awesome about the sheer force of life, as Manson makes us acutely aware in this passage, which also re-creates most vividly for us the life and beauty of the forest at night. But this is also part of the enthralling fairy tale, and we are quite sure that Bercilak is the Green Knight when Enid says he would believe in the supernatural origin of the singing if he ever heard it, and he replies: "You've probably both heard *me* coming back / Late at night after a fruitless hunt." And so on.

V *At Bercilak's Castle: The Temptation Scenes*

Now comes a change in tone. Bercilak builds up the fire cosily and sends a message upstairs to invite Sir Gawain to come down and enjoy it. When he joins them, they all ask him to tell the true story of the cutting off of the head. Gawain has hardly begun when Bercilak takes over from him and tells the whole story in his broadest accent and most Yorkshire idiom, in the manner of, "When our Sam visited Buckingham Palace." It is a gloriously funny account. Gawain is astounded and asks Bercilak how he knows. "Come, lad," says Bercilak, "that's minstrel's tale," and he pretends to think it is all lies. In a passionate rage, the proud young man stalks out of the room, and he means to stalk out into

the dark and icy wilderness as well; but while he is packing his
things, Bercilak sends his man upstairs to tell him it was all a joke
and to apologize—Gawain had told the whole story in his sleep,
says Bercilak. While they are waiting for Gawain to return, Bercilak begins his temptation of Enid to give her a chance to find
and prove the life force in herself. He rather coarsely mocks at the
Round Table ideal of perfect chastity, and when, irritated, she
resists him, he bets her a long pearl necklace that she will be able
to make Gawain break his vow within the next three days before
New Year's Eve, if she tempts him "only a little bit." Enid is still
protesting when the young knight returns, ashamed of his quick
temper; and after some talk, Bercilak tells him that he is going
hunting for three days, but that, as his guest is not yet strong
enough to hunt, Enid will give him books to read. They make a
hunting pact, as in the Middle English poem: every night Gawain
is to tell half the story he has read, and Bercilak is to give him half
his quarry in return. The scene ends with Bercilak, having by
means of obvious winks and broad hints persuaded Una and his
mother to go to bed, blowing out the candle "by mistake" and
leaving Enid and Gawain by the fireside "to chat." This mixture of
comedy, eerieness, and poetry works beautifully on the stage—
every rehearsal was a fresh pleasure to the actors.

The next three scenes of the act, the temptation scenes, are the
most serious and probably the most beautiful in the whole play.
The delicate feeling that develops between Enid and Gawain is
expressed most subtly in language which is always direct, simple,
and remarkably natural and yet exact.

All three scenes take place in Gawain's bed chamber, a small
room, that by contrast with the desolation and snow outside is
made to seem full of color and warmth, partly by the richly deco-
rated screens and tapestry around his bed, but mainly, of course,
by the words. I shall not deal with the story Gawain "reads," some
of which he tells Bercilak on each of the first two evenings, as his
part of the pact. The verse of it is pleasing, properly artificial and
formal to contrast with the spontaneous-sounding poetry of the
rest, and it is full of hidden parallels with what is really happening. These lines, combined with Bercilak's reactions to the tale,
carry hints of Gawain's remorseful sadness about Rosamund, his
struggle to resist Enid, and the rightness of the final capitulation.

The beginning of the first scene is comical. Very early in the morning, to the sounds of the hunt starting outside, Enid comes in in her nightgown; and Gawain in his puritanical way is extremely embarrassed and awkward as she in a joking spirit begins her temptation. But presently she becomes more serious than she had meant to be. She is falling in love, and the tone of the poetry changes with such exquisite tact that the audience stops laughing at the very moment when this begins to happen, and listens instead with attentive sympathy. Enid offers Gawain her love, and he most reluctantly refuses it. But they are both anxious and embarrassed now, and Enid pleads: "Don't think poorly of me: My heart moved me. I had to come / I couldn't stay alone in that cold room / I couldn't with my heart beating in my throat." Moved and miserable, Gawain tells her she must go and she agrees. But she leaves him a book to read with the story in it of a lady whose love was rejected. "Read it with sympathy," she says; then suddenly she forgets herself and thinks only of his fate, "But if it makes you sad, put it away: I want your last days to be gay." And she runs out of the room. The language is fresh and candid, and the feeling between these two inexperienced, vulnerable and honest young people is most delicately expressed in it.

Gawain begins to read and presently falls asleep. Lighting and noises off suggest the passing of the day. Then Bercilak comes in, full of vigor and mockery, with a gift of half the stag he has slain for Gawain, and Gawain tells half the tale he has read, then sums it up as "a kiss refused" and kisses Bercilak in payment. Throughout the whole scene we are made to feel in the background the sadness of Gawain's probable fate and of Enid's—he to be beheaded, she to be bereft.

In the next temptation scene a time-saving device is used, which, by adding a markedly rhythmic quality to the whole, increases the poetic effect. The action takes a whole day from six o'clock on the dark winter's morning, when Bercilak comes into the sleeping Gawain's bedroom with his reluctant wife to try to persuade her to go on with the temptation, until evening when he returns from the hunt. By this time the lovers have fallen very deep in love, and the whole scene is devoted to expressing with the utmost delicacy and force their passionate need for each other in the face of loneliness and cold and coming death. The device I have mentioned is a simple one—it is merely the striking of a bell-tower clock to mark the passing of the hours. The first chime strikes at six o'clock in the morning; the last, at four in the evening. In between, the clock will strike irregularly—say, eleven; and, a few minutes later, two. The effect, apart from its rhythmic function, and the illusion it gives of a whole day passing, is to suggest that the lovers are in an enchanted world where time is not measured by the clock, and that through that enchantment every now and again a warning note is sounded—a warning that Bercilak is to return and that in two days' time Gawain's head is to be struck off.

I quote two brief passages from this scene—the first to show how simply and directly sensuous the poetry is. The long kisses, face blotting out face, the long lingering caresses, now so common on stage and screen, realistic though they may be, leave us emotionally untouched. Our concentration has been broken; we look on in uneasy boredom, a bit ashamed, like spies or eavesdroppers, and we do not at all feel what the characters are feeling. It is something dead and mechanical intruding into the life of the film or play, for we realize suddenly that the actors may even dislike each other. But consider the following lines. The lovers are sitting on the bed:

Enid.   Your hands have hushed the restless wind,
           Your arms feel familiar.   You even smell familiar—
           And friendly.   I can't describe it.
           Do I smell nice?

Gawain.   You are lovely.

Enid.   You can hardly see me.   (*She falls into his arms.*)

Gawain.   I can *feel* you.   A pleasant soft weight in my arms
           And the softest fall of breast and tug of muscle as you
           move.
           I can't describe your smell.   It's warm more than any-
           thing.

Here the natural human small physical details, so simply mentioned, make it all humanly real and full of simple human emotion. Their need for each other is expressed most exactly and without the least strain. The other passage is this; the clock strikes two:

Gawain. Two o'clock on a winter afternoon.

Enid. A weak ray's shining on your armour.
Sh—listen.   Not a sound of the wind now,
The slanting pine shadows will be pointing long strips
Of darkness into the dales.
At three o'clock the streams in the valley beds
Find their way through gloom, through the tree roots
under ice
Towards the still, grey sea.
What a world of movement under the still ice!
How many mysterious things trickle, wind;   roots
through rocks,
Rivers to the sea, underground, unseen;   all moving . . .
Buds into leaf, flower to fruit,
Man into woman, like us here in this dark room, now,
Unseen and unsuspected, growing, putting out tendrils
or hands
To touch and know the power of earth or lover's limbs,
And seek from each the force they need
To open like petals and stretch to the sun.

How wonderfully in every detail this passage expresses the central meaning of the play. The language convinces us that the passion and affection between Enid and Gawain are absolutely natural and real. The Rosamund episode was real enough in its way, but the feeling of both young people there was much less profound. Enid's marriage to the Green Knight, as she explains in some detail to Gawain later has never been quite real, for he is a god. But here, in all the imagery, one is made to understand their emotion, irresistibly rising up, like the sap in the tree, like the swell of the ocean. It is the force of life in them both, the Green Knight force, the mysterious power which works through all nature, in the dark underground, and sets everything magically moving and growing. The way we have been made aware throughout of the cold, still, frozen world outside makes us even more aware of that life that sets the whole world magically moving in the dark under the ice. We have no doubt now that Gawain is right to break his vow of chastity and cleave to Enid even if it does hurt Rosamund: we are made to realize why to act from the center of one's being is more wholesome than keeping to a faded code.

At the end of the scene, hearing Bercilak ride home, Enid flees, terrified. Gawain tells Bercilak he will hunt with him next day and relates to a very ironic listener what more he has read of the story, or rather, experienced, for he has read nothing—his story is a kind of allegorical report of what has been happening. Then he kisses Bercilak on both cheeks in return for half his quarry of a boar.

VI *The Final Encounter*

Act III Scene 4 begins with a chorus of two men reminding us that Gawain has promised to go to his death tomorrow. Today he has promised to go hunting with Bercilak. The shadows made by his candle before daylight loom and stagger on the wall, and the voices comment: "What utter futility. To-morrow he must die, / Yet this is one promise" . . . "And the other? Made to whom?" rejoins another voice. "Who will know or see if he does not go to his doom / Or only half-heartedly searches / For black certain death by cold steel / These thoughts, like shadows, / Loom and reel through his frozen mind / As he dresses himself for the hunt."

Meanwhile Gawain hears noises of Bercilak going off on the hunt without him. When Enid comes in he is at first angry because they had meant to spend the day apart, but instead Enid stays to comfort him. She has brought with her a magical Green Girdle, which was her husband's wedding gift, and she gives this to Gawain, saying it will protect him from death. Not believing this, he nevertheless accepts it as a symbol. After awhile they consummate the love they decide no longer to resist. This is shown not in the usual modern cinema way, but in words that most eloquently make one feel the tenderness, the ecstasy, and the meaning of the physical act. They snuff out the candle; for a few moments the stage is in darkness, till a bell rings five o'clock. Then Gawain gets up and lights the candle again. They discuss the morrow. Enid says she will pray for him, but Gawain says:

> What will happen depends on what you are,
> And on nothing else;

> And what you are will stand in irrefutable evidence
> In favour or against you.

Enid. If God is love he'll understand our sins.

Gawain. If! He is; and must, because he is, judge
And rather send my soul to hell
Than admit a half-baked heart to heaven.

This is one of the many expressions in his work of Manson's philosophy of courage. God demands the almost impossible from us, and we should demand it from ourselves.

When presently Bercilak is heard returning, they have both decided, "no more lies": they will tell Bercilak they love each other. But when he comes in, he demands a story, and when Gawain says repeatedly that he has none, but wants to speak to him, Bercilak beats back his attempts to speak and goes off in a pretended huff, and, with "A fox's tail for you," flings one at him in token of his "treachery."

The fourth act, like the first, though essentially serious, has a delightfully frightening fairy-tale element in it, mixed with fun and humor. It opens with Bercilak's servant Herbert pointing out to Gawain from a ramp above a little dell, where the Green Chapel is—really a cave on the other side of the stream. Terrified of the place, Herbert tries in vain to persuade Gawain to break his promise and finally leaves him alone. As in the medieval poem, a loud sound of some huge blade being sharpened is heard, and Gawain, though terrified, calls to the Green Knight to come out. It is an exciting moment for the audience when it sees him again, emerging from his cave seven foot tall and green from head to foot, with his huge ax on his shoulder. (For the Green Knight's personality is one of the greatest triumphs of the play. His insouciance, his robust humor, his enormous vigor, his North-country accent and countrified manners, his teasing, debunking language, so unexpected in one of godlike powers and divine wisdom and knowledge, make an audience delight in every word he speaks and every action he performs.) "What's your hurry? [calls the Green Knight]. You shall have what I owe you / I've never met a man more keen to collect what's coming to him. Give me time, lad, I'm coming . . ."

An amusing scene follows. The Green Knight teases poor Gawain, who is all tensed up to receive the blow, changing his posi-
tion because the sun is in his eyes, stopping his ax in midair because, as he indignantly explains, Gawain flinched, and so on. At
last, with a tremendous show of force, he brings down his great
ax, then stops it suddenly just as it is about to sever Gawain's neck
and gives him a little nick with it instead. Gawain jumps up,
drawing his sword. "You've had your blow," he shouts half hysterically, and he prepares to fight. But the Knight says quietly "I'm
satisfied," tells him that he is also Bercilak and that he knows all
about what has happened between Gawain and Enid. After a
show (which he thoroughly enjoys) of his immense magical
power to flatten Gawain to the ground or paralyze him at a word,
he demands from him the Green Girdle that Enid has given him.
But Gawain stoutly refuses it because it is a symbol of the love
between himself and her. In a flamboyantly evocative descriptive
speech, full of sensuous beauty in spite of the flamboyance, the
Green Knight summons all the winds of the air to blow toward
him all the waters of the earth, and they rise to a huge crest infinitely high out of sight, where he stops them. The whole stage is
drowned in green, translucent light from them. (All this in production is suggested, of course, by the combination of poetry,
sound effects and lighting.) Then he threatens to bring all this
down on Gawain if he does not give up the Girdle. Gawain defies
him because the Girdle is a symbol, but he does so without hope.
When he looks up the Green Knight is sitting on his upturned ax
blade, "tenderly—amused"! Suddenly feeling that as the Knight
is indeed a great god, he should be revered and not defied,
Gawain falls on his knees, asks for forgiveness, and offers the
Girdle to him. But, taking it, the Green Knight gives it back, saying, "Off with thee lad / Spring on thy Gringolet and scud up the
snow Tha lass is waiting." For both he and Enid have accepted
the challenge life offers and have stoutly resisted their fear of it.
The Green Knight walks quietly away.

This last chorus is a beautiful poem, with a contemplative,
winding rhythm, a little sad, but with a sweetness in its melan-
choly. Its function is partly to explain Gawain's attitude to the
past and the people in it that he has left behind him in facing the
Green Knight's challenge. Especially he thinks of Rosamund,
whose generosity he will never forget. It is indeed a green and

lovely play, such as only a young man could have written—but a young man who was a born poet—a writer with a humane and generous spirit, who had already acquired much wisdom.

Critical reception of the play, both inside and outside South Africa, was cordial. Sir Ralph Richardson wrote of it that the poetry was beautiful and the development showed a genuine feeling for theater. It was dedicated to John Speirs, from whom—a fortnight after the poet's death—a letter arrived including this comment: "To think that I have inspired a play—your play—makes me feel that I've done something in this world! The play itself gives me great pleasure. It has brought the youthfulness and freshness of that time—both of your own youth and of that early age of the world, as it were,—and it somehow brings together the England of D. H. Lawrence and of the medieval English poem."

CHAPTER 5

The Noose-Knot Ballad

*T*HE *Noose-Knot Ballad* was produced by Manson himself in the tiny Cygnet Theatre at Pietermaritzburg in 1956, and some years later an excellent broadcast of it was made by the Canadian Broadcasting Company. Despite one or two defects, imaginative production and first-rate acting made the tragic and poetic quality of the play come over strongly. The famous Scottish actor, John Duncan Macrae liked *The Noose-Knot Ballad* so much that he wanted to put it on for the Edinburgh Festival one year but was unable to get financial backing.

I *Comparisons with Earlier Work*

By the time Manson writes *The Noose-Knot Ballad* he has passed through the youthful phase in which *The Green Knight* was written, and there is a vast difference in the mood and manner of his work. *The Noose-Knot Ballad,* written after a bicycle tour of Northern Scotland and the Shetlands, is strongly influenced by the old Scottish ballad, *Edward, Edward!* The plot and compactness of the tale which Chaucer's Pardoner has learned by rote, to illustrate his outrageous sermon on the text of *Radix malorum est cupiditas,* is an equal influence. Both are bitter tales of violence and greed. In *Edward* there are contrition and remorse as well, and these are strongly present also in Manson's play. The language, like that of both Chaucer's tale and the anonymous ballad, is conspicuously spare and terse. Gone are the fresh candor, the open, free quality of *The Green Knight* speech and rhythms. Instead the spirit is dour and grim, like the religion which has shaped all the characters whether for good or ill. The speech, both of choruses and main text, is the Scottish dialect. The play is short, the characters few. In the first and last of the three acts there are only three people, all murderers fleeing from justice in the mountains; in the second there are Roderick and a handful of people in a village inn.

The play is called a ballad, for it is like one of the ancient traditional ballads in its direct, simple, laconic speech, strong rhythms, emphatic rhymes and near-rhymes, narrative gaps, surprises, and the rhythmical irregularities (like those of sprung rhythm) natural to extempore compositions like the ballad, and natural also in living dialogue, however poetic. It deals, as the ballads do, with basic human emotions: love, rage, jealousy—leading to murder. Ballads have a refrain; the play has three choruses, each a ballad in itself, each stanza consisting of question or answer, and the whole working up to a dramatic climax, as in *Edward, Edward!* The first ballad begins the play, the second comes at its climax, and the third ends it.

The plot is like that of *The Pardoner's Tale,* but radically modified to suit Manson's purposes. In Chaucer, three gamblers find a mound of gold coins in a lonely spot. One of them is sent to the nearest town to buy food and wine for them all, and while he is away the other two plan to murder him so as to keep all the money for themselves. They do this, but he, with the same purpose in mind, has poisoned the wine he brings, and so they all three die horrible deaths. But in Manson's play, only one of the murderers has a hard heart, and though all three die, the story takes a totally different direction to illustrate a totally different moral. The Chaucer tale is a story of heartless greed and the grimly ironic revenge the money they murder for wreaks upon the thieves. Manson's story, on the other hand, is a profoundly sad one about three men, two strongly sexed and passionate (not bad men, radically, but baffled or confused and driven to sudden violence by the conflict between their own instincts and the narrowness of their Calvinist upbringing). The third man is mean, greedy, and sly, but in his life too sexual frustration plays a part. The first two are generous, though wild, and repentance comes to them, but, in a way, too late; the third dies unregenerate. An important "character" is Roderick's *Doppelgänger,* who, the play suggests, may be entirely a figment of Roderick's imagination, but is certainly also his deepest knowledge, or his conscience. His voice is always heard as that of the questioner in the three chorus-ballads, and sometimes it might almost be called the voice of God.

II *Ballad Qualities in the Play*

The play begins dramatically, ominously, with the loud beat of
two drums of different pitch behind the closed curtain, the beat
growing faster and faster like the systole and diastole of a racing
heart, until at last with two very loud beats, they stop. Then two
voices fill the theater, the *Doppelgänger's* relentlessly questioning,
Roderick's answering with pain and reluctance. The *Edward*-like
ballad they speak between them behind the curtain creates a
strong feeling of tension and prepares for what is to come in Act
I.

The ballad also excites interest in the "hero," Roderick, and pre-
disposes the audience to consider his story, now about to be un-
folded, with horrified compassion. For it is clear before we meet
him that the murder he has just done, of an unknown man whose
body now lies in a ditch, was not merely senseless, brutal, or
greedy. It was the result of an irresistibly powerful surge of passionate rage, so strong that it had not spent itself in his first killing
—that of his father—nor is it spent yet. What has set all this in
motion is true and generous feeling on Roderick's part. His father
has ruined and degraded the whole life of the girl Roderick loves
by marrying her "quick" in Roderick's absence "To a dull thick-
brained clod O." It is his bottomless pity and shame for her that
rouse up such a tidal wave of overwhelming fury that he batters
his father to death, and before the madness has had time to sub-
side, he kills a perfect stranger simply because he reminds him of
his father. We feel the danger in him still: anything may happen.

The ballad is a powerful one. Being a dialogue, it takes the
place of an opening scene, and no scene could be more dramatic
or lead the audience more rapidly right into the heart of the play.
Much is conveyed in a few forceful words which, with strong
rhythms, create an intense idea of the hateful, perverting pressure
his father's moral stupidity exerts upon his son; one or two bitter
sentences expose his unforgivable, unseeing, unfeeling tyranny in
all its ugliness. Because he has fallen innocently in love, the ballad
tells us, his father calls him "hot as the devil"; in the last stanzas
we are made to feel how the banked-up heat in the poor frustrated young man's brain erupts like molten lava, wreaking death
and destruction. The last verse contains the sort of dramatic shock
typical of the best ancient ballads. For in reply to the Voice's at-

tempt to excuse the father: "That's hard, but he meant the best, / And who can tell wha's best O?" Roderick replies, taking up that word "best" in a way that brings home to us how, as he recalls what his father has done, a blind rage of indignation seizes him again against his father and against the Voice for suggesting that *such* an action could ever be best, and every feeling but rage is utterly blacked out from his mind: "I thought it best when home I came / I thought it best when I saw her shame / To beat his grey head flat O!"

III *Opening Scenes*

The facts about the first murder having been established and some understanding of Roderick having been evoked in the audience, the ballad ends, and the curtain goes up on a mountain slope, up which three men are desperately clambering to escape from justice. We realize later that they have just met.

So bare is the language of this play that it cannot be acted by men without imaginative force and complexity. The first words make us feel to the marrow of our bones how cold it is—so cold that without shelter they will die of exposure. Peter McEwan, a fat and elderly ex-lawyer with a weak heart, cannot manage the steep climb without help, so Roderick Anderson, a minister's young son of twenty, carries him on his back. Angus Morrison, a middle-aged ex-mercenary, is the third climber. These two are described by the cynical Peter later on, in a cruelly vivid phrase that makes us see what life has reduced them to, as "a hairy rogue w' a mind like a beast / And a mad-dog boy."

Roderick will not let anyone rest; some man is following them, he says; the corpse of his victim must have been found in the ditch where they have covered it with branches. The language leaves us wondering whether there really is a pursuer or whether Roderick's guilt-haunted mind has imagined it. The effect, here and elsewhere, is macabre, as if there were a kind of unseen presence hunting them up in the mountain. Soon Peter is delirious from exhaustion, so they creep under the scanty shelter of a big rock.

There it emerges from their talk that all three men are murderers. For when Peter taunts Roderick with the prospect of being hanged, Angus says, "We'll all hang, Peter, three abreast in the wind!" (The mind that conjures up such a picture is inured to suffering—the phrase "in the wind" on this bitter night makes the

vision infinitely desolate.) And Angus tells how Peter married a
widow for her money and murdered her soon after. Peter is not
much moved by the revelation. His mind, unlike those of the
other two, is entirely on his physical suffering and on the gold of
which they have robbed the corpse in the ditch. He eagerly counts
it: three hundred golden sovereigns.

Presently it is Angus's story that comes out from what Roderick
says: he and Angus belong to the same village where Roderick's
father was minister. It turns out that they cannot take refuge in
the west because Angus in known there. Peter in his cruel jeering
way probes and probes to find out why. Roderick knows the story,
and under pressure, reluctantly tells it:

> A man moved into Angus' house
> While he was away at the wars,
> And he slept in Angus' bed,
> Beside his wife,
> She bore him two bastard brats.

Peter.   Ach, you had a wife, Angus,
         Why didn't you tell me that?
         And you had a little house, eh, Angus,
         Who'd have thought you had a house?

Angus.   I had a house.

Peter.   And your wench, what happened to her?
         Tell me what happened to her?

Angus.   It was a long time ago.

Peter.   What happened to her, Roderick?

Angus.   I strangled her wi' me bare hands
         And I threw her on his bed.

In every part of the dialogue above one feels the brooding intensity of Angus, a man used to solitude and to being hunted like
a wild beast. One also perceives the natural fellowship between
him and Roderick and the triumphant *Schadenfreude* in the way
Peter needles him. It is clear that the wild, fierce Angus, for all his
crimes, is a man who cares deeply about life and about people, as

Peter never could. It is also clear that he has not yet, after many
cruel years, got over the passion that made him act as he did, or
the horror of so acting.

Roderick has had a bitterly unhappy boyhood in the manse.
This has come out in a sort of explosion of intense poetry when
Angus points out, among the lights of a village far below in the
valley, the bigger lights of a manse. "It's even colder now in the
dusk" grumbles Peter.

Roderick. I wouldna' be sittin' there wi' them
        Locked in their bright little cupboard of light
        I wouldna' . . .

Peter. Wait till midnight comes.

Roderick. Still I'd not sit there.
        I'd not sit there by the roaring fire
        And the great wide windows staring out
        Like bright blind eyes on the night.
        Upstairs it's still and the bairn lies chill
        In his ice-cold bed.
        Dreadin' the morrow
        Dreadin' school
        Dreadin' his father's sneers.
        Under the stairs the house-maid shivers,
        Lying awake, lying awake,
        Her eyes fillin' up wi' tears.
        Oh Lord give comfort to those that weep
        And rest to those tha' lie awake,
        Comfort the bairn,
        Send them sleep.

Peter. Where were you born that you pity those?

Angus. Born in the bosom of the kirk.

Roderick. Ay, colder than any crag.

A wild sadness penetrates these bleak words like a bitter wind.
Roderick imagines this manse in the village below to be like that
he was brought up in, with a child like himself in it, and a servant
maid like the one he loved, and his words, to which the balladlike

short lines, rhythmic irregularities, rhymes, and repetitions add a
further intensity, make us realize how his life has been starved of
joy by the father whom he has killed, and how much fellow feeling he has had for the servant maid in that cold, inhospitable
house as she lies shivering and crying in her meager bed under the
stairs. Roderick's revulsion against his father's moral blindness is
obliquely but most vividly expressed in his strangely forceful
words about the windows of this other manse, which stare out
upon the complex, sentient world with "bright blind eyes," seeing
nothing, like his father, of all the delicate, beautiful, mysterious,
dangerous life that is there. His whole miserable childhood is
summed up in those three poignant "dreadin's," "Dreadin' the
morrow, Dreadin' school, Dreadin' his father's sneers"; and the
few details about the servant girl give a graphic idea not only of
her life under his father's roof but also of his own lively and
tender interest in her.

Peter manages to goad Roderick too into telling his story—such
knowledge may be useful to him—but Angus, revealing how
deeply the horror of his own deed has eaten into him, cries out:
"Dinna' y' answer him, lad / You'll want to tell the world, But dinna'
y'answer / Bury it deep, / Let dead dogs sleep / And the grass
grow high." Roderick's need to tell has now grown uncontrollable,
however, "It's a fit night, listen to the wind," he cries, "It's a fit night
for it all!" He tells the story of the maid who worked in the manse
and how he loved her because she laughed often. "I found it hard
to laugh in that house," he says.

How bitterly he says these last words! "Later I learned to
laugh," says Roderick; and the poetry recreates briefly one delightful innocent day when his father was absent and he and
Jeanie spent happy hours "tickling for trout, like bairns do," and
"ran back all the way, laughing." "When he came back that night
my father looked black as death," says Roderick; he accused him
of wicked lust and packed him off "to stay wi' (his) uncle Bruce."

IV   *First-Act Climax*

Suddenly the scene culminates in the following extremely dramatic and moving climax. By this point a very profound sense has
been built up of the wildness of the landscape, the wild wind, the
desolation of the black night, and the lost passionate sadness possessing the two outcast men. Roderick cries out:

It's a wild night, it's a wild night, Angus,
The wind shrieks in the grass.

Angus.   Roderick, Roderick, stop your story!
Bury it, it's past.

Roderick. Three days ago I threw open the door
(My father was at his desk)
Where's Jeanie? I said.
Unless you tell me I'll have you on the floor,
So help me God, I was shaking, Angus,
I'll have you on the floor!
Ah, Roderick, said my father, sit down, take your rest.
Sit down, now listen here, Roderick,
I've done what's clearly the best . . .
Wha' ha' y'done to Jeanie?
She's married, boy, that's wha' I've done.
Tha's wha' I've done!
Tha's wha' I've done!
That's what I've done, Angus,
And my God I'll do it again!

Angus.   I canna' hear, the wind's raging—I canna' hear a thing!

Roderick (*shouting*). I'll do it again. I'll do it again!
Can you hear that quite plain?

Angus.   Shut your mouth!

Roderick. I'll do it again.

Angus.   Shut your mouth or I'll cut you down
And blackness take your soul!

Roderick. The night's as pitch as hell.
There's hell for ever for you, Angus,
There's hell for ever for me!

Angus.   Hold your tongue!

Roderick. I'll not hold my tongue now, Angus,
Not for you or any man!

Angus.   Then I'll stop it wagging for ever.
I tell you, hold your tongue!

Roderick. Draw your sword then, Angus,
                It's a fine black night for your death!

Angus   (*drawing his sword*). Right then, Roderick, my bonny,
                May the devil take your breath!

(*They begin to fight savagely with swords. Peter hops around
them, encouraging first one then the other.*)

Peter.   Cut him across the eyes, Angus!
                In his ribs, Roderick!

(*There is a sudden blinding flash of light, both men reel, and the
thunder comes like an explosion—and dies away rumbling down
the valley.*)

Angus   (*stepping back and dropping his sword*).
                Holy Lord Jesus!
                Your eyes shone like stars!

Roderick. I saw my sword and my sword hand
                Raised above your head.
                Beyond there was a thin black cloud like a bat's wing!

Angus.   The devil's wing! Ach, crazy visions!

Clearly, it is the anguish that shrieks inside Roderick's soul as
well as the wind that shrieks in the grass. Angus cannot bear Roderick to speak of the murder. "Bury it, it's past!" he shouts above
the wind, but he cannot bury his own horror—even after all these
years—and he is terrified that it will attack him yet again. By
these very simple lines in the total context the poet compels us to
feel for both men. It was the girl Roderick cared about—the light-
hearted creature that taught him to laugh. By rushing her into a
marriage with a "clod," his father, Roderick believes, has quenched
her happy, innocent spirit and irreparably spoiled her life.

How complacent and hateful his father seems to him at that
moment is powerfully expressed by the smug, dull rhythm of the
fragment of his father's uneasy, rather guilty speech that he recalls: "Ah, Roderick, said my father, sit down, take your rest/Sit
down, now listen here, Roderick / I've done what's clearly the
best." A terrible rage suddenly and totally overwhelms Roderick,

and when he comes to himself, he finds, quite unrepentantly, that
he has killed his father—"beaten his grey head flat, O." The sud-
denness with which this happens, the fact that it is done before he
has time to realize his own intention, his feeling that his father's
act has infinitely more than deserved the murder it reaped, and
the knowledge that his murderous rage has not yet (even after his
second murder) spent itself—all this and more is compressed with
tremendous poetic force and quite startling dramatic effect in the
balladlike ellipsis of the following lines:

> Wha' ha' y'done to Jeanie?
> She's married, boy, tha's wha' I've done
> Tha's wha' I've done!
> Tha's wha' I've done!
> That's what I've done, Angus!
> And my God I'll do it again!

By this time, what with the black night, the shouting, the raging
wind, his own pain cruelly reawakened by Roderick, and a rage of
obstinacy in both men, Angus has become so infuriated that a
fight spontaneously breaks out. Though of different generations,
they have both been brought up in the same religion, and both
believe in hell; for both of them Roderick's despairing words have
a deep literal truth: "The night's as pitch as hell/There's hell forever for you, Angus / There's hell forever for me."

Then comes another intensely dramatic moment. Something
happens, but exactly what is kept mysterious. There is a flash of
lightning, a tremendous crash of thunder reverberating down the
mountainside, a strange visionlike cloud—and all at once a
change of heart takes place in both men. Simultaneously they realize that they do not want to kill each other but are only mad with
cold and hunger, and they decide amicably that Roderick shall go
down the mountain to the village, where he alone is unknown, to
buy bread and cheese, with wine for Peter, Burgundy for Angus,
and whiskey for himself. As he goes down, Angus thinks he sees a
man following Roderick, but Peter, seeing only one figure, says,
"Mist makes men look double sometimes." The audience are sure
that Angus has seen the *Doppelgänger*.

V *Village Scenes*

The second act contrasts strongly with the first: instead of the wild, cold mountain ledge, it is a simple Highland village inn, warm and sociable, with a handful of people drinking in it, and in a dark corner an old deaf-mute sitting, almost hidden in the shadows. There has been a shout of laughter, for two half-drunken crofters, Jamie and Donald, have been telling of an unnecessary fright they had. Into this pleasant company walks Roderick, exhausted, wet through, nerve-racked, and taciturn. He accepts the drink that Jamie offers him but seems much troubled by the figure in the shadows. "I think he's waiting for someone," explains the hostess, Mrs McAlister, and the words have a sinister ring. The audience suspect that the figure is his *Doppelgänger*.

Talk centers in the murder that has happened that afternoon, and as Roderick listens in silent horror, he hears that the victim, one Robert Gunn, was a desperately poor man, against whom Fate, as Jamie, in a fit of maudlin pity, expresses it, had "ganged up": sickness, hunger, death, the failure of his crops had dogged him for ten years, and the three hundred pounds of which Roderick and his two companions had robbed him had come, he now learns, as an unexpected legacy. Stricken to the soul by this news, Roderick is faced with the fact that the man he has killed was a human being and one with a sudden late chance of happiness. He is tortured by this realization; and the drunken postmortem sympathy of Jamie, for a man he had obviously never helped when alive, becomes unbearably galling.

Then he learns from a constable who is there that he and his fellow murderers are trapped; the soldiers are waiting for them at the bridge which leads to their only possible escape route. Hastening then to buy the food, wine, and whiskey he has come for, Roderick is just hurrying out of the door when he almost collides with two men carrying a stretcher on which lies the sodden corpse of Robert Gunn! At the sight of his exposed face, Roderick faints, and Mrs. McAlister and the rest cluster around to help. Here again, as in *The Green Knight,* Manson uses a device to express something more briefly, intensely, and dramatically than could ever have been done by conventional means: while all the other figures on the stage pause in whatever action they are performing, frozen into immobility, the deaf-mute in the shadows, who now has a devil mask over his face, walks forward. Roderick rises slowly to his feet as if in a trance, and the second ballad of the play is spoken between him and the figure in the devil mask, who speaks with the same voice as that of the questioner in the first ballad, Roderick's *Doppelgänger*. Well produced and well acted, this double movement—the confrontation of these two—has a thrillingly impressive effect. The simple words they speak, both question and answer charged with Roderick's deep-felt, almost heartbroken sincerity, are all the more effective for the balladlike, irregular, unpolished, almost extempore form of the verse.

The poetry reveals the revolution that has come about in Roderick's soul. His fit of violence has (no doubt during the cold, solitary descent of the mountain in pouring rain) at last spent itself. His heart was never hard, as is shown by many things: his attitude to Jeanie, his carrying Peter pick-a-back up the steep climb, his comradely sympathy for Angus, his pity for whichever "bairn" and "maid" are living in the manse he sees lit up in the distance. Now when he hears the pitiful story of Robert Gunn's life, and especially when he actually sees the blood-bedaubed corpse of the man he has murdered, it is not surprising that he is so shocked into contrition that he loses consciousness. But his mind has been working fast, and it is clear from the ballad that he means to warn his companions that they are trapped and to try and convert them to repentance so that, though their bodies cannot be, their souls at least may be stayed from dissolution. Roderick has, after all, though he found the bosom of the kirk colder than any crag, been brought up in the Christian faith. The intensely vivid phrases of contrition, such as "my beast-black brain" and "sin's sick domain," make us feel how unspeakably hateful his state of violence and guilt has been to him. He is very young and he has some hope of winning the other two to a clearer and calmer state of mind before they die and of saving them from hell.

The same heartbeatlike drums as in the first act have been sounding all through this ballad. Now with two loud beats they stop, and the masked figure steps back into darkness; the people on the stage all begin to move, and observe that Roderick has recovered and is on his feet. Mrs. McAlister tries to persuade him to stay the night, but he is more anxious than ever to get back, and as he goes out of the door, the deaf-mute, now without the devil mask, follows him. "Poor old man," says Mrs. McAlister. "He must have given up waiting," says the constable.

VI *Violence on the Mountainside*

The third act opens on the mountainside again, where Angus and Peter are awaiting Roderick's return, Angus brooding over the past and Peter plotting for the future. From what the two men say, our knowledge of Angus, our compassion for him, and our sense of tragedy are immensely deepened. Angus talks of getting a job once he is safe and of starting a new life: "D'you think new clothes will change your character?" taunts Peter. "Dogs and mobs have hunted you over these hills / Wind and rain stain the skin, Angus / But the mob yell and the dog howl / Burn right down to the brain."

The effect of this intense language is increased by the patterns of sound. Peter's pitiless words evoke pity: such brief phrases, with their powerful monosyllables, as "the mob yell and the dog howl," re-create the horror of the kind of experience Angus has survived again and again: "yell," his terror at the sound of his human hunters, dehumanized by hatred and excitement; "howl," his terror at the cry of his animal hunters, savage by nature, and trained to use their savagery on fugitives like him.

Angus, like himself, is "a surviving man," says Peter. All that matters to Peter is survival and the money to achieve it with—if only he could have half of Roderick's share as well as his own. But while he is trying to direct Angus's attention to the idea of murdering Roderick, Angus is wholly absorbed in quite a different matter. In the course of fifteen lonely years, hunted like a wild wolf in the mountains in all kinds of weather, he has had time enough to consider what was really happening the night he murdered his wife.

> I've had plenty of time to think of tha'
> In cold hours on a moonlit night
> Or a rainy night under a rock
> Or a dripping tree.
> The wind howls,
> The moon scuds for shelter in the clouds
> Or drops down,
> And the coldest hour of dawn descends . . .

We are made to feel acutely the solitude, the desolation of spirit in that, to know the weather, and to see the scene. The sparse words are charged with meaning, for the lives Manson describes are, in Conrad's words, "informed with passion, possessed of convictions," and therefore more poignant and real than those of many actual people. Angus sees now that it was the scandal-mongering neighbors, clustered around his house on the night he came back, watching him, avid for sensation, who confused him and gave him no time to think:

> They didna' tell me she thought I was dead . . .
> (*to himself*) Oh, Peg, Peg, did you think I was dead?
> (*to Peter*) She tried to speak, I think, Oh, Peg!
> My fingers made her throat so small
> Not one wee cry came out at all . . .
> Until she fell back.

Peter tries to reawaken his jealousy by saying sourly "On the bed?" But Angus is lost in sorrowing retrospect. "Ay," he says, ". . . there was a wee sigh . . . but then she was dead."

> There was something gone in my head . . . (*he goes on*)
> (*to himself*) Oh, Peggy, Peggy, did you love him, girl?
> Did his hair curl?—I didna' see—
> And was old straight-haired Angus dead?
> Ah, but you wept for me, Peg I know . . .
> Better if I had died,
> If you had cried for what was true
> Than I should have come back to you
> Wi' murdering hands!

These few brief words make one realize strongly what happened in Angus's mind when he murdered his wife fifteen years ago; at the same time one feels the huge change that has almost suddenly taken place in him as the culmination of his years of solitary brooding. Flustered and confused by the old women gathered around his house and hissing him on like geese in their envy of love and youth, he felt no check within him then to the surge of murderous rage and righteous jealousy that overwhelmed him at the sight of his own bed that another man had slept in— and of the children his wife had borne to that other man. At last, however, he has learned to see it all differently. He recalls vividly the exact detail of how he killed her, but now he sees the deed from her point of view almost as if he were physically the woman: "My fingers made her throat so small/Not one wee cry came out at all." He gave her no time to explain that, as he discovers later, she had thought him dead; now, with the deepest self-blame, he thinks with agony of that "wee sigh" that was her last breath and that seems now so pitifully small a protest against his huge misdeed.

Angus, like Roderick, is a strongly sexed passionate man capable of powerful feeling about the woman he loves. This feeling has been wrenched out of its natural course by repressive influences and has led to murder, for the salacious attitude of the old gossips has driven Angus into a rash assumption and a headlong deed. "A proper play you put on for them, Angus," jeers Peter, with his unfeeling cunning, but with a truth that nevertheless sears Angus's soul.

Manson treats even Peter with understanding as partly a victim of repressive Calvinism. But though on the surface quite a pleasant, sociable sort of fellow, yet, as the plot grows more and more complicated, he emerges as an utterly heartless materialist. Wanting the money to be divided among two instead of three, Peter tries in vain to persuade Angus, during Roderick's absence, to murder him when he returns with the bread and wine (which Roderick, in his exalted mood, feels to be symbolic). Yet Angus's mind is unconsciously poisoned, so that shortly after Roderick appears he stabs him to death on a sudden, mistaken impulse. A moment later he repents, but it is too late. Roderick is dying, attempting with his last breath to warn them about the bridge, but he is dead before he can get the words out. "I've done it again," says poor Angus flatly, and the words strike upon the ear with a profoundly tragic sound.

Peter, however, callously drags Roderick's body behind a rock and settles down to drink the whiskey the victim has brought. (This, it will be remembered, was the drink that Roderick was to buy for himself. The others had chosen wine, and Peter does not doubt, judging Roderick by himself, that the whiskey alone is unpoisoned.) Angus, dazed with grief, and knowing that Roderick was incapable of poisoning anyone, drinks down both the other bottles. Delighted at Angus's rashness, which he is convinced will soon leave him the sole possessor of all the money, Peter taunts him with his folly, expecting him to die at any minute. It is Peter, however, who turns pale and begins to tremble and stagger. Presently he doubles up in agony, clutching his heart. The play has given many indications that Peter is ill with a failing heart. Moreover, he is old and fat and suffering badly from overexertion. Peter, however, immediately assumes that Roderick had meant to commit suicide and poisoned his own drink. He still hopes for survival, however; in his very death agony he goes on plotting: while Angus, at his pathetic request, is trying to pray for him with his eyes closed and his back turned, Peter raises his dirk for a fatal stab and, in the very act, falls down dead.

Now Angus is left alone in the freezing night, with only the candle inside the lantern to keep back the darkness. He cries out, "Wha' in the name of darkness Does all this horror mean?" In the visible, palpable world there is no answer. But the play finishes with a final chorus, which does produce in the end some kind of answer, one not without beauty and not utterly without some kind of light or hope. The same voice that spoke to Roderick speaks now to Angus out of the blackness broken now only by a faint glimmer from the candle. And when the chorus ends Angus drops the lantern, the stage is plunged in darkness, and the curtain closes to the sound of a mounting wind.

VII   *Interpretation*

Angus will die very soon, we know, in darkness and solitude; his last uncertain answer to the Voice, however, has shown that out of all the wild sadness of the events we have witnessed, something of incalculable value has been gained. It has come partly from the human fellow feeling between Roderick and Angus. For the Voice in the last chorus, which is the voice of Roderick's *Doppelgänger*, his deepest knowledge, is now speaking, as it were, from the almost subconscious depths of Angus's mind. When confronted with the corpse of Robert Gunn, Roderick had felt to the full the horror of what he had done, and after that he had cared for nothing but to help his two companions to a similar cleansing realization. That they were all three to die soon did not seem to him important in comparison with the huge importance of truly realizing the evil that one has done and being truly sorry for it—simple words for the most thorough revolution that can transform a human being.

When Roderick is killed in his muddled attempt to bring this about, he seems to be defeated almost before he has begun. Yet though Roderick and Peter are both dead now, Angus has learned from Roderick's generosity—for his penitent grief, his attempts to save the others, both proceed from generosity. This generosity, falling like a blessed light upon Angus's almost unbearable consciousness of his own wrongdoing and wrong feeling, enables him, the ballad shows, to struggle through his despair and at perhaps the last conscious moment of his life (as his last words in the ballad show) to feel some kind of positive belief in life—in God, some might say, or in mercy. For Angus, as for Roderick, the hopeless cycle of violence which the repression or perversion of good and natural feelings had set in apparently uncontrollable motion, is at last stopped. It does not matter that neither of them will ever be able to act out the change any further. The change itself is a happening—it happens in their minds, or perhaps one should say in their souls, for there is no other word to sum up the whole of the inner life. It is the ability to feel generously and naturally again that in both their cases has "saved" them. This is clear from the whole progress of the play, and it is made even clearer, by poetic means, not by moralizing, in the last ballad-dialogue.

Answering the Voice, Angus cannot believe that fire (the fire of repentant suffering) "burns out sin, O," as the Voice has said it does, and there is a touch of the obstinacy of despair in what he says:

> *Angus.* No, sin burns for ever and ever,
> No, sin burns like acid forever,
> Fiercer than candle flame, O.

> *Voice.* Let it eat your heart then, what more's to be said,
> Angus Morrison,
> Let it eat your heart then, what more's to be said
> Only you yourself can say, O.

> *Angus.* I repeat that wha' I've done, I've done
> I repeat that like a hollow drum,
> Wha' I've done, I've done, O.

The obstinacy is there still, and it cannot be dissolved away except by himself, but the influence of Roderick (as it were), represented by the Voice, goes on working within his spirit: the warning Voice speaks the penultimate stanza with its strangely moving internal rhyme:

> *Voice.* The wick is spluttering, the night is shuttering down,
>   Angus Morrison,
>   The wick is sputtering, the night is shuttering down,
>   And what is done is done. O.

As the Voice repeats this last line, the words have taken on a different meaning. When Angus says "And what I've done, I've done, O," blank despair is reflected in the flatness of his tone. But the Voice now turns the words so that they catch a different and an infinitely more hopeful light: "And what is done is done, O." "It is finished, Angus," the Voice seems to say, "and done with. Now be at peace." And after a pause, Angus is at last able to accept this:

> Done long ago, ay,
> Done long ago, yet what else can I cry
> But mercy on all men who die
> And snuff out like candle-flames in a night, O!

There is some mercy somewhere in the universe, he feels, to which he can appeal, and his death is no longer meaningless to him.

It may seem strange that he should say "Done long ago" when it is so short a time since he killed Roderick. But it is the cycle set in motion with the murder of Peg fifteen years ago that he is thinking of, which has led to all the acts of violence of his life—a cycle similar to that working in Roderick when he cries after his second killing—"And my hands still itch / To kill another man, O." This cycle and its stopping are the theme of the tragedy, a theme relevant to South Africa, which has long been familiar with the kind of Calvinism Manson deals with.

The Noose-Knot Ballad is a beautiful, powerful play, as grim as *The Green Knight* is happy, and with dialogue as laconic as that of *The Green Knight* is free, and "easy as the leaf grows on the tree." This play is quite as poetic, but the poetry belongs to a totally different mood. The craftsmanship is admirable: the whole play, with its balladlike sound patterns and rhythms, ellipses, surprises and roughnesses that give an extempore air, is almost as much a ballad as its three ballad-choruses are. It is also eminently actable. There is quite enough external physical action in it to provide the hungriest actors with meat for stage movement. Occurring actually on the stage there are a killing, a duel, an attempted murder resulting in the sudden death of the would-be murderer, a dead body brought into a room and causing violent shock to everybody there, a delirium, a swoon; and there are hints, culminating in one physical appearance and two vocal emanations, of a mysterious ghostly presence. What more in the way of what is vulgarly called "drama" could a producer wish for? But, immeasurably more important, expressed through everything that is said or happens, there is an inner drama—inner conflicts, inner crises, and eventually, inner victories, full of grief and suffering—of the kind we call tragic. What play that has ever endured has lacked that kind of inwardness?

CHAPTER 6

The Counsellors

MANSON'S next play, *The Counsellors,* is a strange one for so young a man to have written, for its theme is corruption, and its most important characters are four old or aging generals— Karinzin, Hundrad, Blanker, and Zwartin—and one aging dowager queen—Diomedina. They are the five Counsellors of the title. Among them they try to wield power by influencing the young King, Dioran, chiefly through the two women whom they unscrupulously throw in his path, Gentia, the Queen's protégée, and Saffrona, the Generals'.

The play (a five-acter) has recently been printed by the Natal University Press and was produced in 1964 by the Natal University Dramatic Society. I shall discuss it here as briefly as its complexity and interest permit. In the 1964 production, Mr. Jacques Berthoud was the producer, and Manson himself took the role of Blanker.

I *The "Exposition": Opening Scene*

Time and place are left vague to give scope to the theme. Some heroic, half-barbaric age is propounded, some grandeur of background. The Actor-Playwright (part chorus, part character) opens the play by describing briefly in pithily beautiful verse the remote, wild landscape in which the audience may imagine the story.

In this first scene, the exposition, the Actor-Playwright speaks from in front of the closed curtain, until the characters waiting behind it to play their parts, lose patience, and burst in upon him angrily. He then introduces them to the audience (invisible to them). They are the five Counsellors, and the ten-year-old boy King, Dioran, crowned that day, for his father has just died from a horse-kick. He had been a great man, conqueror, and administrator. His story, says the Actor-Playwright, was

83

> . . . as old as the hills:
> The success of Barbarian arms,
> The wealth, the power, the new provinces . . .
> Proud empires ploughed in
> And the new earth,
> Fertile with the dung of past decay,
> Ready for the seeds of the next civilisation.

Now the whole process has been halted. The passage quoted here illustrates the tone of the play. The people in it will bear huge responsibilities; there will be grandeur and magnificence; there will also be blood and corruption and, one senses, a need for heroic action.

The characters begin quarreling, the Actor-Playwright probes and questions, and the coming struggle for influence over the young King is foreshadowed. The Queen accuses all the Generals of having been flattered by the dead King's giving them power into "serving him like slaves." They were all brilliant men, who should have fulfilled themselves, each according to his own gifts and nature—Karinzin as a poet, Hundrad as a philosopher, and Blanker as a farmer. But instead they have all become the soldierly King's Generals to please him; by so losing their integrity they have started the corruption that is the theme of this play. It will be centered, we perceive, chiefly in Diomedina and Karinzin. Karinzin, we guess, has been Diomedina's lover, and is now so devil-ridden by guilt that he is determined the kingdom shall be ruled as the dead king would have ruled it; Diomedina is so obsessed with hatred of her dead husband, and of Karinzin for having deserted her after his death, that she is hell-bent on its being ruled dead against their wishes. The child Dioran seems likely to be torn to pieces between them. (We learn all this with extraordinary rapidity.) But the scene is brought to a dramatic close by Zwartin's suggestion that the Actor-Playwright may be a foreign agent; the characters advance angrily upon him, and he saves himself only by calling for the curtain, which comes down in the nick of time.

The Actor-Playwright has a useful role: as a chorus he saves time, and Manson uses him often to hint that the imaginative writer cannot always control his characters: they may become so real that, knowing better than he does (as it were) what they would do, they take over. After this dramatic and intriguing "false start," so to speak, the Actor-Playwright announces that the play proper is about to begin, exactly eighteen years after this first scene. Returning from huge conquests, the young King has just arrived in his capital to sit for the first time upon his throne there.

II *The "Play" Proper*

It is a strange play, at first seeming sodden with guilt. The King and his Generals unflinchingly take full responsibility for the crimes and cruelties of the bloody war just ended. But all are haunted men: their guilt comes initially from power-greed, which presently focuses in the two young women they exploit—who, by being used, are tainted too. Finally Dioran, smelling the secret corruption and sickened by it, half guesses, half discovers its source. He has the courage to act ruthlessly; then the guilt-sodden atmosphere clears; in fact, the last scenes of the play have a peculiar radiance and clarity.

The play proper opens in an anteroom to the palace banqueting chamber. It is clear from the noises offstage that Dioran's young officers are extravagantly celebrating their victorious homecoming. Hurrying manservants, disheveled girls, and an old servant called Chromis cross the stage. Fear almost paralyzes Chromis when four young Brigadiers—Sanger, Gules, Erithus, and Rufus —come lurching in, ridiculously drunk, searching in absurd places for their friend the King, but going off, easily distracted, to swim instead. It is all very lively and amusing, but the drunken young men seem as dangerous as gelignite lying around. When presently the King appears and then his mother, Queen Diomedina, enters, Dioran tells her that his overstrained war-weary men need to relax for awhile. He seems almost obsessed with compassion for his four Generals, now his Counsellors:

> I've watched old soldiers in their beds (*he says*)
> They thrash and thrash and cover up their heads.
> Sometimes they cry out,
> Shrill, like eagles, in their sleep,
> Sometimes they mutter;
> Once or twice I've heard them weep.

And again he speaks of how they "sob in their sleep"

And in their waking hours
Roll and finger their past failures
And present depravities round
Into a globe of dirt
Like dung beetles do.

His language about them is full of intense images, which express
their suffering, and his complex insight and disinterested sympathy. The one about the eagles makes us see the hook-nosed, withered, lean old man, lonely in their high positions, authoritative
and courageous but cruel too: they have torn living things to
pieces and are likely to do it again. In the dung-image, full of
disgust, the wearisome rolling movement of their dirty absent-
minded fingers is imitated in the rhythm. And yet, beyond the
disgust, one is aware that Dioran feels their heroic qualities and
much remaining sensibility.

Queen Diomedina is distressed by her son's brooding melan-
choly and proposes to cheer him by sending a clever young girl to
talk to him that evening. At this point, the Brigadiers rush in full
of a scheme for a battle with broomsticks between two of the
Brigades at the Victory Games that afternoon. Manson's young
Brigadiers contrast vividly with his aging Generals. They are like
the young in *Sailing to Byzantium:* their words and actions give a
happy impression of attractive, reckless high spirits, youthful
horseplay, and a positive delight in danger.

Next comes a brilliant little scene between Diomedina and Karinzin in a rose garden while the Victory Games are going on. The
complex love-hate relationship between these two powerful
people emerges subtly and clearly. Diomedina accuses Karinzin of
meaning to gain power, by using Saffrona to allure the young
King, and it dawns on him that *she* means to use Gentia in that
way. The whole idea of using women so (though he is later to
adopt it himself) is so revolting to Karinzin at this stage, that he
cries, "Go. Hide from the sun. You disgust the daylight," and with
these scalding words, he departs. Diomedina, still defiant but
weeping with anger and shame, tears the roses in her hands to
pieces as he leaves her.

Into a hilarious scene that evening, in which the Brigadiers,
very much the worse for the broomstick fight, are rolling on the
floor, howling with laughter at the sight of one another's black

eyes, bruises and missing teeth, comes Gentia, sent, as promised, by the Queen. The Brigadiers, with many suggestive remarks, "tactfully" remove themselves. At first Dioran and Gentia get on well: Gentia, who is clever and learned, has been reading with Dioran's former and beloved tutor, his father's friend, old Cantathes, and this is a bond between them. But, in Gentia's talk, we scent the Queen's secret and relentless plotting against the influence of her dead husband, and as Dioran smells, as it were, his mother's influence on Gentia, he dismisses her brutally with these gibing words:

> How rotten sweetness stinks!
> One can get used to it.
> But Kingdoms sink I think
> When Kings can't tell
> Sweetness from foul smell.
> Isn't that so, my sweet?

His manner is almost violent; many different things are present in his language: not only the nausea and staleness caused by drinking too much and the haunting horror of his war experiences but also the troubled groping of his mind; nothing around him is clear and honest, and the innocent Gentia is suspect. This is shown by his so jeeringly calling her, when he has just made the word so questionable, "my sweet."

III Act Two: The Generals

The *business* of the second act is soon told. In the first scene the four Generals agree at an all-night sitting to win Blanker's daughter Saffrona over to their purposes. She, as her father says, could make any man mad, and if Dioran fell in love with her, through her they could defeat the Queen and gain Dioran for their own plans. In the second scene Zwartin, whom Saffrona has taken as a lover out of pity, works upon that pity to make her take on the task of influencing Dioran.

But the *texture* of the act is rich, complex, and constantly poetic. In it our insight into the "wicked old men" and our sympathy for them are greatly deepened. Though, at first, the talk of the Generals seems obscure, very subtly, from the interweaving of thought and feeling among them all, we learn to understand them

all better. What they agree to is horrible, toward Saffrona, toward
Dioran, and, in one way, toward themselves, for of course they
hurt their own souls in the process. Hundrad and Blanker especially feel the wrongness and the danger. But none of them, except Zwartin, are radically bad men. Karinzin is the driving force.
Hag-ridden with guilt about his personal disloyalty to the king
when alive, and bent on opposing at all costs the Queen whom he
has deserted, he drives the others into his own obsession. Whenever Zwartin speaks, it is to support Karinzin—but Zwartin cares
only for power. Hundrad and Blanker consent because (we realize) they are both too absorbed by their personal inadequacies to
attend: weaknesses that have grown upon them because they
have injured their integrity by serving the old king for power.
They have not enough integrity left now to resist the passionate
driving force of Karinzin.

Yet we perceive their virtues. Karinzin, though set like adamant
against the Queen, is still a true poet full of human feeling. He
understands Hundrad; he feels for his wife; he knows what ails
Blanker. But in his fanaticism a genuine attempt to achieve something good by a certain means has become a blind obsession with
the means. There is something noble about Hundrad, but he is so
sunk in abstract thought that he can no longer communicate feelingly with men and women, and in a way he has become a fraud.
As the scene goes on he is deeply troubled because his wife is
dying, and he "cannot regret her death." He cannot bear the fact
that, "kind and good soul" as she is, a person of great "moral intensity," she does not seem to think that, with all his thought and
word spinning, he is fully a man; and so she has deliberately
chosen to separate herself from life: "She does it herself," he says,
"Secretly day by day,/Slipping away—willingly—/Into that awful
dark."

Blanker is a man of great warmth and natural feeling, a man
who knows the earth and natural things. He was born to be a
farmer, but, when "times were rough," became a soldier instead
for the sake of power. So he has deteriorated: "You remember
how strong I used to be, Karinzin?/Now I'm like an old sack/
Mouldering on the granary floor." That simple image "sack," with
"granary," makes us imagine him easily heaving sacks of grain on
to wagons; the idea of the wheat inside them makes us feel something natural, wholesome, and essential ("the staff of life") in

what he was and what he used to do; "mouldering" suggests the disease, the corruption by disuse of something good and whole-some. His tragedy, and partly the cause of his corruption, is that he so passionately loved his wife, who left him for another man, that now his feeling for his daughter, Saffrona, is unnatural, a mingling of something almost incestuous with aversion. And so he has grossly neglected her. He almost hates her, and this troubles and shames him.

In what he says about Saffrona, in intense poetry, we are aware of a rich beauty, a naturalness like Blanker's, in her and in her wild mother; there is a hint of her being a wild creature too, with a drop of her mother's bad blood in her, and we are made to feel how Blanker cannot help blaming Saffrona, as it were, for the agony the thought of her runaway mother and his unconquered passion for her make him suffer. Blanker ends by washing his hands of Saffrona: "Why should I worry who jumps her?/She may throw good, she may throw bad/A king or a pimp—who can tell?"

Zwartin says little, but we become aware of a certain cold inhu-manity in him: the dying and death of Hundrad's wife, for ex-ample, which so deeply stir the other three, do not interest him at all; he is untroubled by all that, and he obviously seizes upon the weaknesses of the others and secretly uses them for his own ad-vantage.

It is impossible to describe this interesting and complex scene adequately in the space available. There are some strange touches, showing that the three older Generals are by no means extroverts—they were born for other things. When, for example, Hundrad is about to leave for his wife's deathbed, Blanker says to him, taking his hands in both of his own: ". . . take this touch . . . / The far-gone, like beasts and children / Can tell the friendly touch." And later when the cock crows, Blanker and Ka-rinzin both know for certain that Hundrad's wife has died at that moment.

It is only in the blazing light of the next short and brilliant scene, however, that the full extent of Zwartin's cold-hearted du-plicity is exposed to us. In it we see him deliberately using the far too softhearted Saffrona's pity for his pretended shame and grief to make a tool of her. "I sleep with the King," she enquires, "and you control him?" But, she says, what if I fall in love with him? Zwartin, however, knows how to deal with her. From pretended jealousy and anger he passes to pretended pathos. "My strength depends on you, Saffrona," he pleads, "That's the truth / Proud Zwartin's sunk to a pimp/In his old age." And sinking his head in his arms, he appears overcome with shame. Deeply moved, she puts her arms around him but leaves when he asks her to. No sooner is she out of the room than Zwartin sits up cheerfully and shouts to the servant for his breakfast. And "fold back my bed" he commands, "I can afford to sleep."

IV *Flashback Scenes in Acts Three and Four*

At the beginning of Act III, the Actor-Playwright unexpectedly intervenes again. He will, he says, compress the next six months into a series of flashbacks and so give the audience "Terror of truth/In no more than the halt/Or the missed beat of a heart/And remorse/The seeming everlasting ache of remorse/In a sigh only."

The emotionally vivid poetry foreshadows the sad and passionate experiences that are to come. The actors he calls up are bound, he says, to tell him the truth, "however much it hurts." This is another of Manson's comments on the mysterious processes of wholly serious imaginative writing. The Playwright calls Dioran to question him about the past six months in front of an audience of strangers. "Is a man's sick heart a spectacle," protests Dioran vehemently, "To be shown for a penny a peep?"—but he has to answer.

Seven intensely poetic and powerfully dramatic brief scenes, five of them in Act III, follow in a sort of dream or vision sequence, played on an almost bare stage. Only the most fragmentary idea of them can be given in the space allowed. What emerges with considerable and most painful beauty is that Saffrona and Dioran have fallen very deeply in love with each other, but that somehow Dioran becomes more and more clearly conscious of the corruption present in their passion, though he cannot know of Saffrona's affair with Zwartin, nor of Zwartin's exploitation of her love for him (Dioran) to gain the General's political ends. Yet Saffrona, out of weak pity and too easygoing good nature cannot give up Zwartin. Gentia too is in love with Dioran who, without loving her, has promised her marriage. She naturally feels betrayed when she discovers the affair with Saffrona, and consequently Dioran suffers bitterly on her account and on his own. But a certain pettiness of character in her, which is what has made it possible for Diomedina to use her in her turn, makes it impossible for Dioran to make her his Queen. He ends, cruelly enough, by renouncing both women and is left in a state of bitter cynicism and misery, having sunk down in dejection on some steps in the palace and apparently fallen asleep.

The device of making the whole thing so painful and shaming to the actors in retrospect (when they are forced to reënact it publicly) has a powerful effect. For by it we are made to feel strongly for all three, and the depth, turmoil, and complexity of feeling that have to be experienced by human beings who care ("not to care," says Dioran, "is a crime") are communicated to us in poetic dialogue of remarkable force and vividness.

The next scene, which is a strange one, as if not quite of this world, but of unearthly perceptions, begins in a very realistic manner (as if the seven scenes just dealt with had been a dream of Dioran's). The day breaks; the servants go about their early duties; and the four Brigadiers, whom Zwartin had sent off on various missions to be out of the way, are back in the palace, shouting about the rooms, and looking for the King. From the gossip of the servants, and the disrespectful talk of the Chamberlain, it is clear that there has been a great deal of dissipation and disorder and that the haunted Dioran has been leading a notoriously intemperate life. Suddenly Dioran rouses himself from where he lies on the steps, and the servants flee, but he calls back the good old man, Chromis, who used to be Diomedina's special servant, and who adored the old King. "You are his living image," Chromis says to Dioran. "His image," exclaims Dioran ". . . like this?/Like a tearstained child?" "He could not sleep either, my Lord," answers Chromis.

Shocked by the revelation of his father's similar unhappiness, Dioran begins to question the old man, asking whether his father thought himself wicked, or was deceived by any one near his heart. For this is his own situation, he feels. Chromis hesitates, and before he can reveal her secret, Diomedina, who has come in unobserved, stops him. Karinzin hears the whole conversation unseen.

First Diomedina reproaches Dioran harshly for his behavior to Gentia the night before. He refuses to apologize. "We were both too ugly then to look at one another," he says. He has bad dreams, he says, and a deeply disturbing passage follows. He dreams, he

says, of a lovely garden, with people walking up and down in it.
Suddenly one of them

> Will stab someone walking side by side with him
> And not stop in his step,
> But link his arm with another
> And neither looking down, walk on,
> Leaving that poor bubbling thing
> Red in its blood
> Under the rhododendron . . .

Diomedina. That is a drunkard's delirium!

Dioran.   . . . But other laughing couples come,
> See what is done
> And pass without a word—
> Laughing—like everyday people do!

Diomedina. Drunken horrors and nothing more!

Dioran.   The dream goes on
> Until those walkers one by one
> Have trod that bleeding face into the grass—
> And then I wake.

All the terrible guilt feelings with which so much of the first three
acts is infected come to a head in the poetry of this wonderful
symbolic dream. Dioran, being a king, feels acutely though ob-
scurely the guilt of his subjects—the Generals, Diomedina,
Saffrona, Gentia—he is conscious, almost as if it were his own
guilt, of the taint in all of them.

The language of the dream, almost unbearably vivid, like a
nightmare or a hallucination, is heavily loaded with moral horror;
the sense of betrayal of friend by trusted friend contained in its
images is full of a kind of incredulous abhorrence, as if the
shocked dreamer rubs his eyes: can he really be seeing such un-
speakable cruelty, such unfeeling acceptance of treachery? And,
of course, Dioran is feeling his own cruelty to the two women, left
to suffer because they love him, which makes him feel, however
irrationally, that they too have been betrayed, and by him. But
there is no help for it. The images that express these complex feelings, dark and confused as the feelings are, are appallingly vivid

and clear: "Leaving that poor bubbling thing"; "Have trod that bleeding face into the grass."

Diomedina, however, is flinty-hearted toward her son. She commands him to apologize to Gentia, but he refuses: "No, mother, that would start it—/All that dark again!" "Your father had these fancies too," says Diomedina impatiently, "Sitting all night with a bottle between his knees." And suddenly an obscure knowledge inside Dioran begins to grow clear, and he turns away from her and speaks, apparently into the empty air:

> Father . . .
> Does the dark press down on you still?

Diomedina (*horrified*). Dioran!

Dioran.   No, mother—leave me—leave me—
I must look . . . into my mind . . .
Something turns there . . .
Like a belly of a fish in the dark.
God knows what it may be . . .

By sheer intuition he has almost guessed the treachery that haunted his father's dreams; and as he turns to speak to his dead father almost as if he were there, Diomedina runs off in terror.

At this moment Karinzin stirs; seeing him, Dioran calls him to come forward. Karinzin, like Diomedina, now knows that somehow or other Dioran sees clearly that he has betrayed him. He has overheard what Dioran said about his recurring dream, and, deeply ashamed, he confesses, "I have caused your dreams." In reply Dioran says quietly "Dismissed," and Karinzin, like the great soldier and poet he is, knows that there will be no reprieve for him. He takes the silver star, "for Courage," from his breast, and offers it to Dioran. Though inexorable, Dioran is deeply sympathetic. "Keep it," he says, "That was won in the shadow of death. . . ."

But as he is going out, Karinzin has a very brief sort of stroke or fit, in which he believes that the old king speaks to him from the dark of death. This heartens him; he is able to get up, and he makes a short, poemlike farewell speech to the effect that one must laugh at suffering as if it were a joke, but though that is brave it is mad: suffering is terrible too; and he ends:

> Conduct yourself with dignity,
> For that mad laugh is a terrible thing,
> A man's death is a terrible thing,
> The corruption of youth
> A terrible thing,
> A lover's or a wife's contempt is terrible,
> And a king's contempt . . . unbearable . . .

So he goes out. All the terrible things this play shows us he could bear, but not the contempt of a king, a true king in all the full implications of the word—a king like Dioran's father, or a king like Dioran. By the time we have reached this point in the play, we realize that Dioran, in his ability to take responsibility, has indeed become a king, like his father—kingly, but not merely in his father's image. Karinzin goes out, to die, we guess, by his own hand. Almost heartbroken, Dioran tries to call him back, but in vain.

V *Mystery of the Dead Counsellors*

The fourth scene of the fourth act takes us wholly by surprise. It is four days later. The Brigadiers are sitting about in the Generals' Committee room, waiting for the King, and as soon as they begin to talk, we gather that all the five Counsellors are dead. The Brigadiers do not know why this has happened or how, except that Hundrad has left a note saying that Karinzin and Diomedina took poison and that Blanker killed Zwartin and was mortally wounded by him; it is obvious that he himself fell on his sword. We guess at once that Dioran has discovered the Generals' plot to influence him through Saffrona and that they have felt (all except Zwartin) that the only way out with honor was a self-inflicted death.

The young men discuss the dead Generals with great admiration. Old Chromis comes in to replenish the wine decanters, and it is obvious that he is confusing the distant past with the present and believes that everything is as it was about twenty years ago. As they are talking, Dioran appears in the open door, but nobody sees him. Poor Chromis, on being told that Karinzin is dead (Chromis assumes in battle or by accident), is so distressed about what Diomedina will feel that he inadvertently betrays that she and Karinzin were lovers and is horrified at his slip. Sanger swears him to secrecy: the King must never know. But of course Dioran has heard. Pretending to come in for the first time, he enters and tells the Brigadiers he has promoted them all: they are now all Generals. "We cannot take their places," says Sanger, "but we can do their jobs. We are not fools." And indeed the whole play has made us realize that. Then, seeing that Dioran is tired and distraught, they go out. So the scene and the act end with enough of the corruption cleared away for Dioran and his young Generals to make a new and hopeful start.

VI *Fifth Act*

The fifth act is nearly all a kind of flashback. Dioran is left alone on the stage. As he goes up to Karinzin's empty chair and speaks to him and to his mother as if they were there, it is clear that his mind is dwelling on the deaths of his five Counsellors. He is a king among men, and though he has had the strength to dismiss from their office, and so, in effect, from life, the five revered and close associates who were using him for their own ends, his mind is full of understanding and compassion for them. Here again the device of the Actor-Playwright is set to work. He comes in, chagrined because the play is still obscure, and Dioran, now decisively in command instead of the hesitating Playwright, orders him to "make sense—somewhere." Pulling himself together, the Playwright then deferentially summons Diomedina from the dark of death, and, after a pause, Karinzin comes too, both ghostly looking until the Playwright commands a lively lighting. The scene that follows, in which they reënact their double suicide, is one of the most moving scenes in the play.

They are full of remorse for the way they have blighted Dioran's life. This makes them feel acutely how old and ugly they have become; and, moved by mutual pity and sorrow, they embrace, all their old love for each other returning. To comfort themselves they begin playing an old game familiar to them as lovers: closing their eyes and imagining themselves going on a journey high in the air and describing what is below. It works for awhile; then suddenly the enchantment is gone, and they feel old and ugly again. The Playwright jeers at their childishness. But Dioran's heart is rent at the sight. "Look at her! What is she pretending to be!" sneers the Playwright, but Dioran cries, "Young again! Only young again!" and he calls out passionately to his mother; but of course she can't hear because she is dead. Then Karinzin says, "I

have it here/The cure for sick souls," and he shows Diomedina the
bottle of quick poison he has brought with him. Agonized, Dioran
calls out again and again to her not to drink it, but when Diomedina realizes that Dioran may learn of her infidelity to his father,
she cannot bear the thought of facing him, and she almost con-
sents. "Mother, Mother, You need not tell me . . ./Mother, hear
me!" shouts Dioran in his impotent anguish. Almost as if in this
ghostly form she does retrospectively hear him, Diomedina starts
violently. "Why did you start? What is it?" asks Karinzin.

Diomedina   (*perturbed*). It was as if my heart—or something—
              Moved inside me for a second . . .

Karinzin.   What?

Diomedina. You would not know—as if my womb stirred . . .
              Or something kicked against my heart! Oh Karinzin!
              (*she weeps*)

Karinzin.   What is it? Please! Don't cry! What is it?

Diomedina. I am ill, old—yet something stirred in me . . . as
              if . . .
              Oh, Karinzin! They are children! Just children!
              She is only a child,
              A lovely laughing child . . .

Karinzin.   Who?

Diomedina. She is as soft and sugar-spiced as her name is.

Karinzin.   Saffrona! Oh! A honey-brown child!

Diomedina. All golden children by the sea-shore in summer.

As this vivid and suddenly tender memory comes up in them
both—in Diomedina's case part of it is even antenatal—they seem
to realize (the poetry suggests) at the very core of their being
what it means to have used and corrupted youth and innocence—
people who were once beloved and familiar children—and they
seem so ugly to themselves, and blame themselves so bitterly, that
Dioran cries out again and again in an agony of pity to contradict

them and to remind Karinzin of such things as his weeping at the
death of a boy soldier. "Remember!" he cries, and Karinzin starts
as Diomedina did, remembering Gentia suddenly with the same
vivid tenderness as they remembered Saffrona, as a little girl of
two or three or so, with "her funny little face." Again they feel to
the full what they have done; though both are afraid of death
(the brave Karinzin has always sweated with fear before a
battle), both decide to take the poison. Dioran watches with
agony, shouting vainly to them to stop. There is something almost
unbearably poignant in the complexity of this tragic spectacle.
They are dead, and he has virtually ordered their deaths, but they
were people whom he has loved and admired. "It's such a pity
. . . a pity, a pity," he cries, "They are not really ugly, you can
see." But the Playwright, who has become very unsympathetic,
answers with sarcastic irony. "They were not *really* ugly! I see."
They *were* ugly of course, and the King had to bring their crimes
home to them, "to set it right." But there was a beauty in them
too, never quite extinguished, and Dioran feels it with helpless
pain.

Diomedina drinks first, for she will not let Karinzin leave her.
"Not again!" she cries, and as she drops dead, clutching Karinzin's
hand, he asks:

> What were you trying to warn me of
> That your fingers dug so into my flesh?
> That there is nothing there but darkness?
> That I've always known, my dear . . .

And he drinks the poison and dies.

"Well, do you want more?" asks the Playwright, but Dioran has
no stomach for more. "Why should I pry into their secrets?" he
says, "Let them be at rest at last/Poor distressed souls." But suddenly the ghosts of Blanker and Hundrad appear unbidden. But
when Dioran bids them speak since they *are* there, they talk to
each other like the old friends they always were. Hundrad bitterly
feels himself to have been, with all his brilliant gift for abstract
philosophy, a fraud; he is desolate because his wife knew it, and,
though she loved him, he was glad to be free of her moral intensity when she died. Blanker suffers because he neglected his
daughter, simply because she looked like the beautiful defaulting

wife whom he so extravagantly loved. While they are talking they
hear Zwartin in the dark corridor going toward Saffrona's room,
and the truth about his debauchery of her suddenly flashes upon
Blanker's mind—and on the watching Dioran's. Blanker draws his
sword and goes out into the dark passage to meet Zwartin. There
is a scuffle and a cry; Blanker comes back, clutching his bleeding
side. Zwartin is dead; Blanker manages to stumble to a chair, and
Hundrad with trembling hands pours him a glass of wine. But it is
too late; he falls forward on to the table, dead; and, after a pause,
Hundrad draws his sword and lays it on the table, sits down, pulling a piece of paper toward him, and begins to write the note that
Sanger read aloud to the Brigadiers at the end of the fourth act.

But Dioran refuses to look any longer and walks forward. The
curtain closes, leaving Dioran alone on the stage. The Counsellors
have not talked of remorse or repentance in this scene. They have
not expressed sorrow for the evil that they have done, but (all
except Zwartin) they have resolved to die, for, having fully recog-
nized their evil, they suddenly feel free of it. It is Blanker's very
deep affection for his daughter, which he has suppressed because
he has suspected it of being incestuous, that overwhelms him
when he guesses what Zwartin has done, and enables him at last
to do his duty by his neglected child. These three—Diomedina,
Karinzin, and Blanker—do not need to talk; they merely act. But
Hundrad, the philosopher, has to think things out, and when he
has told the tale to posterity with proper decency in his brief farewell note, he too is free to die.

VII *Final Scene*

The last short scene begins with these words from Dioran:

> I know you lie behind my back, Hundrad,
> Quite dead,
> The cold steel in your guts,
> Do not despise me if I cannot look upon your death
> Even though you came to act it out for me.

The curtain softly opens behind him, revealing an empty stage.
The Counsellors are all dead, and no one knows for certain exactly how they died; and yet, the Playwright and Dioran agree,
they might have died so, as Dioran, in the "pondering and won-

dering" of "sick thoughts late at night," has imagined. For the last two scenes have shown what Dioran has imagined. "I felt the sense of it all, I think," he says. "Come, then, let's end it," says the Playwright. "End it?" exclaims Dioran, "No, there's still fight left in me, you'll see./Try if you like, try to dismiss me" and, though the Playwright calls for a curtain, nobody obeys. Dioran then summons his servant and the Chamberlain to draw the curtains, which they begin to do. "And pull back my bed," commands Dioran, "It's time to rest my weary head." The Playwright stands disconsolately watching the curtain drawn. Then he shrugs to the audience and walks slowly off.

This play is very different from the three already completed. It seems to me heavy with poetry as a loaded tree is heavy with thick foliage and ripe and beautiful fruit. It has a dark, rich quality, quite unlike the simple, clear lucidity of *The Green Knight,* or the tense, harsh, sad beauty of *The Noose-Knot Ballad.* And the poetry of course, is never a mere decoration, as in, say, Flecker or Christopher Fry. It is in the very veins and arteries of the play itself.

CHAPTER 7

The Festival

*T*HE *Festival* and *Captain Smith* originated as one as yet untitled play. At the stage where a royal pair are hiding behind a fallen tree from the revolutionaries hunting them down (Act II, Scene 2 of *The Festival*), Manson introduced his mad Captain Smith; he became so fascinated with developing this strange, charming, yet (in the circumstances) terrible character, that the middle of the play grew out of all proportion to the rest. As a consequence, Manson became so alarmed about the probable length and about the rapidly dividing aim of his play that he could not go on. He therefore neatly excised the whole of the Captain Smith part, continued and finished the rest of the play without him, and then returned to Captain Smith. Thus, there emerged two separate and quite independent plays: *The Festival* and *Captain Smith*.

Though the King and Queen and Duke Brandel of the two plays bear the same names, they are not the same characters. Those in *The Festival* are developed in one way; those in *Captain Smith*, in another. For though a writer's intellect may plot a book, his deeper intelligence may create characters which, coming alive, take over the story and change it. The two stories have each an entirely different course and bearing. *The Festival*, roughly speaking, is about idealists, on the one hand, who can be quixotically brave in the pursuit of an ideal and expect other people to be the same, and more ordinary people, on the other, who do not want to be great but only happy in the comparatively narrow way familiar to them: the play shows with complete sympathy that both points of view are valid and interesting parts of life. *Captain Smith* has a totally different theme. It is a true tragedy about an exceptionally good and brave man who, simply because he is mad, places three other people in an insoluble dilemma (insoluble dilemmas are common in real life). This one is never solved, but it is ended in a most moving way.

I Action of the Play

The Festival was produced at the opening of the new theater of the University of York, England, in 1968. The play consists, essentially, of two stories, the first taking place three hundred years after the second, and in some ways similar to it. The main thing that is proclaimed and rejoiced in by the people in the later story —what, most simply, the festival *celebrates*—is the significance of the similarity between the two stories and the way in which, by a generous use of the imagination, the living can learn from the dead. Both stories are important and absorbing, but the heart of the play is the older one, the play-within-a-play. As I wish to attempt to do justice to the passionate depth and complexity of this central drama, I find myself obliged to deal very briefly with the other, more "recent" story.

The play takes place in mountainous terrain. We find ourselves near the top of a deep ravine which forms the boundary between two countries. A rope bridge across this ravine has just broken, flinging men and horses to their death in the rocks and rushing waters far below. A most vivid description of this terrible event, given in the opening lines, sets the mood for the play and provides an image and a symbol which recurs again and again.

We meet various characters: a group from the other side of the ravine, who were about to cross the rope-bridge when it snapped— two rather thoughtful peasants; a mean merchant and his sensitive wife; an imaginative and lively Bard, Robert—and King Edmund and Queen Isabel, rulers of the country in which the action takes place. All are shocked at what has happened. The King offers compensation, and the Merchant attempts to get more of it than he deserves. Suddenly the Merchant's wife and the two Peasants remember that it is their festival day. The three of them, helped out by the Bard, explain the meaning of their celebration to the King and Queen: it is a festival of life and death, at which the dead are honored and their deeds, whether famous or infamous, are seen truly and accepted creatively as a part of the essential pattern of life. "Sweet sense," as the Bard says, is made out of "life's disorder." At such a festival, clearly, the principal celebrant is the poet or bard, for it is through art that patterns and unities are perceived.

The King discovers that the Bard has written a play that he had hoped to have performed at the festival, and, on the insistence of the others, he asks the Bard to tell the story of it. The Bard explains that it is about Robert, Duke of Brandel, a great and dashing nobleman from his own country, who exactly three hundred years earlier had traveled with a King Edmund and a Queen Isabel, ancestors of the royal pair who are on the stage; Brandel had fallen when the rope bridge was broken. It is, as the King says, "a strangely fitting story."

It soon becomes clear, however, that the story is a traditional one in the Bard's country and that there are different versions of it. Before the Bard can begin, one of the Peasants chips in with *his* version, in which Brandel is pictured as a dastardly villain. The Bard objects to this as a popular cheapening of the tale and of the character of the hero, and he feels it is his solemn duty to tell the tale truly. But the King and Queen, who question the Bard closely about his poetic trade, begin to become hostile to him: they sense that the imaginative power that he claims somehow represents a challenge to their own, and they also suspect that the Bard's version of the tale will be less to the credit of their ancestors (with whom they instinctively identify themselves) than the Peasant's has been. The King, who is utterly bewildered by the Bard, becomes contemptuous and meanly vindictive toward him. The Queen, on the other hand, is annoyed with him partly because he fascinates and impresses her. A delicately complex relationship develops between her and the Bard. He is wholly dedicated to his poetic vocation and believes passionately in its value; he sees himself as the transparent medium through which imaginative truths find expression. The Queen responds ironically, with a woman's common-sense skepticism about things which seem to her rather unreal: she seems genuinely unable to accept the Bard's belief, and yet there is some dishonesty in her denial too.

In Act I, Scene 2, they are all preparing to sleep in the forest. The King again becomes angry with the Bard, whom he considers arrogant, and in a burst of temper he throws the Bard's notes for his play into the fire near which they are all sitting. The Queen and the others are horrified; but, pressed on by his rage, the King strikes the Bard and has his soldiers truss him up and throw him into some nearby saplings. But before this is done, the Bard has shown the King that by behaving in this way he has put himself in the Bard's power; he has also warned the King, mysteriously, that even though the notes for the play have been burned the truth will out: the people in the play, who are long dead, will somehow speak through the mouths of the living, and they will do so that very night. The King is scornful of the idea, but the Queen is in some awe of it.

At this point, where the play-within-the-play starts to form, the action calls for somewhat fuller discussion and analysis. The past comes upon us gradually. The Bard comes upon his meaning—or rather, meaning comes upon him, and upon the other characters, and upon us—in slow stages. *The Festival* pictures the very working of the imagination, the gradual laying bare of "the life of things."

At the beginning of Act II, scene 1, the Bard is lying trussed up—his *body* is completely confined—among the saplings, at the back of the stage (he remains there throughout the scene); the King and Queen are asleep under the roof of a woodcutter's shack. It is night. On to the stage—as if into the dreams of the sleeping King and Queen—limps Robert, Duke of Brandel, dressed in black, maimed from his terrible fall; he is, the stage directions tell us, "the same man who played the part of the bard in the scene before."

Brandel comes to the King, who wakes up, afraid, taking him for Robert the Bard. When he realizes that it is a ghost who is speaking to him, the King protests that he is alive; but Brandel contradicts him:

King.   . . . Look I am living!

Brandel (*indulgently*). Are you?

King.   Look! (*he slaps his face and limbs.*) Alive!

Brandel (*his patience gone and suddenly angry*).
            God almighty, man! What sort of worm are you?
            Who dead as I am
            Done, dug in, rotted for ten generations,
            Cannot look a fellow ghost in the eye
            Or socket he uses to see with?

> Has your spirit even no dignity at all?
> Must it squirm still? Pretend
> You, unlike me,
> Have not felt the worm turn in the foul flesh?
> And cried that all you were—or could be—
> Has come to carrion?
> If only for that last miserable unreality,
> I know you are my Edmund!—dead Edmund.

King.   I'm not! I'm not! I'm alive—I swear . . .
        (*His last word dies rather dismally on his lips—as if there*
        were some doubt in his mind.)

Brandel (*calmly*). Better be dead.
        For if you are that living Edmund
        A dead man hides inside your head
        And you and he are one!

        (*A sudden change comes over the King. His voice*
        changes, his manner changes, and his attitude to Brandel
        changes; he speaks, in fact, with the voice of the dead
        King Edmund who exists so strongly in the living Ed-
        mund's consciousness that it looks to the audience as if
        there are two men in his body.)

In the previous scene, the King has already taken the part of his
ancestor. But it is also the *death* within him—his lack of generosity and of kingliness—which forces him to succumb and become
the dead man. Still, it is through this transformation that he plays
his part, although unwillingly, in the festival of life and death.

In the dialogue between Brandel and Edmund I, the old story
begins to take shape. Immediately it becomes clear that Brandel
acted bravely and that he was betrayed by the King and in some
way also by the Queen. His actions were heroic:

Brandel. . . . I dare not even look at her
          Lest I forgive what no man should . . .

King   (*angrily*). Should do, should do! It's always that with
                      you,
                 Isn't it, Brandel—what you *should* do?

Brandel (*bleakly*). Ay, what else can you do but what you
           should do?
           What have you but one short life?
           But given it again,
           I would do—what I did do.
           And you would give a thousand lives
           To do what you did not do, Edmund.

King. Would I?

Brandel. You betrayed me once before—
           Would you do that again?

King. I could *not* cut
           My world away from beneath my feet . . . for noth-
           ing . . .

Brandel. Nothing?

King. *What* for then?

Brandel. So that she could be—a Queen . . .

King. A Queen? Her? Ha! Ha! Ha!

The fall from the bridge, we see, is at the very center of the battle
of souls fought out so long ago. The King is clearly an ignoble
person, but he is not unintelligent; and these words of his have
some power. Brandel's magnificent gesture (whatever exactly it
was) seems to the King to have been partly inspired by a bleak
fanaticism, a self-righteous dedication to abstract things, which
may have limited the generosity of what he did. We are reminded
of the Bard who has shown a wonderful and earnest self-
confidence. And the coming together of the two Roberts is significant in other ways: the poet (it suddenly strikes us as inevitable)
is the equivalent, on a different level of experience, of the noble
hero and adventurer.

Brandel died so that Isabel could become a queen. But, we
learn, she refused his challenge, came back to a husband she despised, and lived out her life with him in horror; and now they
"mew and cry out in the night," "each to the other / Complaining
how close to each other and forever/They must lie." And Brandel

is in despair: his death achieved nothing; even the words which
he shouted to Isabel as he fell were not heard:

Brandel.   As I fell . . .

King   (*incredulous*). You spoke? Said what?

Brandel.   I tried to . . .

King.   What? Not comfort her?

Brandel   (*rather taken aback*). . . . I meant some comfort . . .
            But rock and iron-hard water
            Hit sense and breath from me first . . .

King   (*with a touch of disbelief but also genuine admiration in
            his voice*). Oh, you are crazy! CRAZY!

Brandel   (*firmly and didactically*). She would never have learned
               from you . . .

King   (*bellowing*). What she *should* do?
            (*more calmly*). And you could tell her with words, could
               you?

Brandel.   She *saw* me, falling,
               Make it plain—that mankind *can* do what it should
               do . . .

The contrast between the coward and the idealist comes out powerfully in these lines. Brandel is admirable (and he is vividly created, undeniable for all our Prufrocklike nervousness about heroic
sentiments). Yet our view of him must be in some ways similar to
the King's: does not Brandel's profound and astonishing humanity
become, in the end, somewhat *in*human?

One by one, the facts and feelings of the old story are suggested
or hinted at. The King tells Brandel that he thought—and that the
Queen hoped—that Brandel would wish to marry her. But Brandel explains (what the King already knows) that the law of their
land forbade even the first peer of the realm to consort with
queens: "She and I have known that from childhood." All that he
could offer her was his "undying loyalty," to "death if need be."

Brandel abides by what he believes to be right, with complete
fidelity; but again—the question is implied—is such a law, and
such fidelity to it, somewhat unnatural? The King thinks so; so did
Isabel, whose ghost, the king tells us, hates Brandel.

Brandel   (*suddenly getting angry*). Hates me! But why?

King.   How can you be so utterly . . . inhuman!

Brandel. Haven't I been honourable?

King.   Oh, Brandel . . .

Brandel. Haven't I?

King.   Scrupulously honourable . . .

Brandel. And didn't she—deliberately—refuse to become a
            Queen?
            Wasn't my country ruined forever
            Because she would not be?
            Did I die for nothing? fall for nothing?

We begin to become aware of the precise nature of the clash of
personalities which took place, three hundred years earlier, between Brandel and Queen Isabel. Since then, she has suffered
from remorse; and to Brandel, all seems a waste: "What is the use
of all man's suffering?" He says to the King, as the latter falls
asleep:

            You have no guts,
            I have no heart, apparently,
            And she, poor misery, has no honour
            And must be equally indifferent to us both . . .
            But—why does that still anger me?

He has begun to understand what happened, but nothing is properly explained or in its place, and he is still angry.

And then the Queen—it is Isabel II—awakes. She too at first
takes Brandel for the Bard, but she has been dreaming the things
that we have seen and is horrified when the figure before her
points to the Bard lying inert in the saplings:

Brandel. Yes, it is me!

Queen. Brandel! No! Oh no! no!

Brandel. Yes, poor Brandel.

Queen. No, I'm dreaming! Go away, go away!

Brandel. I cannot . . .
That young man there who moans and turns
In a river of sleep
Has summoned me.
He shivers and cries in the dawn-cold air
And dreams . . .
Of Kings and Queens . . .
Sometimes his dreams of them have come so near the
    truth
That some ghost-figure stirs in death
And mumbles half-alive a line—or less,
Betraying some trick or mannerism of speech
Which gives the poet power over him.
If he achieves it so unerringly
That his words *are* what we have said,
What can we dead men do then, pray,
But act our real parts in his play?

Brandel's speech describes not only the benevolent power that the
Bard has over him but the exciting hold the play may well begin
to have upon the audience. The Bard suffers and dreams, but the
boldness of his dreams accomplishes an unexpected truth. It is
interesting to consider that it is its unashamed dreaming—and the
meaningfulness, the *accuracy* of it—which gives *The Festival* its
power and makes it so remarkable in the midst of the postwar
crop of *tranches de vie* and plays of "the absurd." The combination of easy movement and formality in the last lines of the passage quoted above makes us realize that the Bard's struggle "in
the dawn-cold air" has been successful but also that it is through a
magical *ordering* of reality that poetic success is achieved.

The Queen tells Brandel that she is alive, for all his insistence
that she is just like the dead Queen; and she orders him to go. For
a moment it looks as if the Queen will manage to resist the Bard's
power; and Brandel cannot understand and master her as he could

the King. But as Brandel limps away, "grotesquely— / Slowly down into the dark—like a twisted toad," the Queen takes pity on his deformity and, though Brandel has by now bravely begged her to let him go, by an act of imaginative generosity she becomes the dead Isabel. It is significant that the woman has been moved by the man's wounds.

Isabel I (as the King has warned us) is bitter and disconsolate. Brandel, on the other hand, shows that the picture we gained of him in his conversation with the King was an incomplete one:

Brandel. Tell me what happened . . .

Queen   (*flatly*). When?

Brandel. After I fell, Isabel. Tell me.
How did the hours and days go by?

Queen.   Like a winter night,
Long and never-ending, Brandel . . .

Brandel. Oh, that we both know, Isabel . . .
Tell me of the summertime . . .
Were some summers sweet? . . .
Were you burnt nut-brown? Oh Isabel!
Did you ride through wheat fields ever—
Trampling them down?
(It's wrong, I know, but did you ever?)
And were they golden-bright?
Was there light and air all round?
Oh, you laughed and laughed!
Or did you sigh
To see the high wheat rippling round you in the wind?
The sweet West wind!

Brandel's values are clearly based upon an alert appreciation of living, not upon any pious rejection. But his enthusiasm still gets no response from Isabel: "My sunlit years were as dull as death!/ Dull! Dull!/What is life but waiting for death?" This bitterness soon becomes anger, as it was bound to:

Isabel.   Let me hear *you*
With your few years of experience of it

Tell me what was so wonderful in life.
I saw it all out
Till horrible senility
Made a dribbling fool of me.
Everything's clean cut for you . . .
And we, who cannot see it clearly,
Are inferior, aren't we?
(*Brandel does not answer.*)
Aren't we?
Yet given your conviction, anyone—
Anyone, low or high
Even he or I   . . .
Could be a hero too . . .
And live in Elysium!

Brandel   (*with a blaze of temper*).
Be silent, woman, you disgrace yourself to speak like
that!

Queen   (*pleased to have angered him*).
Listen to him! Listen to him! *Still* the same!
Disgrace myself? . . . Disgrace . . . a word . . .
But you can't even bear to *hear* it—can you?

Brandel.   Not from you. A Queen must not . . .

Queen.   Disgrace herself?
But I did, didn't I?

Brandel.   You didn't even try to be . . .

Queen.   A Queen? For whose sake? Yours? Ha! Ha!

Brandel.   There are some things that are bigger than ourselves . . .

Queen.   Listen to the slave speak! I am a Queen.

Brandel.   No, you are not, but you could have been.

Queen.   I did not *want* to be!

The Queen's plight is ironic and very sad. She has ended up with
a disgust at life; yet in her disagreement with Brandel she clearly

felt herself to be a representative of warm and vulnerable *life*
against his "conviction," what seemed to be his abstract delight in
being a hero. "Disgrace myself? . . . Disgrace . . . a word. . . ."
The faint memory of Falstaff's contempt for Hotspur is not irrelevant. Brandel seems to be noble, and he despises those who cannot
make his pace. But in reality, she says, his heroics and his enthusiasm are cheap, and he is a slave to his own ideas. *She* is a
queen—mistress of herself and wife to a king (for the moment
she forgets that these two implied assertions have to be qualified)
—though not the queen that Brandel had imagined in his mind.
In Brandel, on the other hand, we detect an awe and a humility, a
passionate dedication to the right order of things—or to the right
order as he conceives it. The dialogue is fierce and pregnant.

Brandel tells Isabel that he spoke to her as he fell. She is horrified and impressed but tries to sneer at the gesture. Brandel's
manly sincerity comes back at her:

Queen. Doesn't every common little hero know that sort of
        trick?

Brandel. Trick?

Queen. Suspending knowledge or belief in death
        For a second or so!

Brandel (*passionately*). You must not say that!
        You may have been on the brink of death,
        So near, perhaps, your foot may have dislodged a
           stone . . .
        And seen it fall.
        But stepping backwards from the brink
        You cannot say:
        "I think it's nothing at all to fall,"
        Or afterwards, "I *could* have jumped . . ."
        Jump or don't jump! Know you did or did not!
        Don't say it's nothing . . .
        For I know it is not!

Queen. You know everything, don't you, Brandel?

Brandel. Everything about falling, Isabel,
        From beginning to end!

And Isabel is overcome by remorse and grief. Her distress answers
Brandel's; and the new closeness they feel helps them to plumb
their enmity more deeply and more honestly. Isabel speaks now
not from any false pride or self-will but from the bitterness of
experience:

> Queen.   . . . And I wept all night . . .
>   And in the morning . . . everything was exactly the
>   same . . .
>   Despite what you had done.
>   Nothing happened . . . no-one came . . .
>   I realised I was alone . . . with what?
>   A notion!
>   How far you fell the day before . . . !
>   For what?
>   For nothing, Brandel . . .
>   I heard myself laugh that out loud . . .
>   For nothing! Nothing!
>
> Brandel. Don't, Isabel.
>
> Queen   (laughing and crying hysterically now). It seemed so
>   silly!
>   All alone with a notion
>   On that bare, high mountainside . . .

Brandel knows everything about falling, but he does not know
everything about not falling. We suddenly see that Isabel's feelings are in their own way perhaps as deep and as right as Brandel's. The grief, the feeling of extraordinary usualness, the need to
apprehend a thing physically before it has any meaning—all this
comes across forcefully. And it becomes clear that Brandel has not
only failed to take into account a part—and an important part—of
human nature but that he has perhaps even evaded something by
falling. There is in her a sort of imaginativeness that he lacks:

> Queen.   Oh, you don't know despair!
>
> Brandel. Don't I?

> Queen. No!—Or what it is
> Not to feel
> Or care
> That the one you loved the day before was dead!

For Isabel, despair is not so much a lack of hope ("hope" hasn't much meaning for her) as a lack of lively feeling.

Brandel has worked out what Isabel's role as Queen ought to be, but he has not seen that it has not become something real for her. "Why try to make me what I'm not?" she asks; "Why should I be your pet Queen,/And believe implicitly what you believe?" Brandel is somewhat cowed. He begins to realize that he and Isabel "live in different worlds": the very voyaging onward which he constantly desires for himself is to her the imposition of a theory upon the reality she knows so intimately. Brandel states what the difference between them is and says that now he need feel no more grief. But Isabel loves Brandel, and he loves her, and each must therefore feel that the other has betrayed their love. The Queen's anger flashes out deeply, terrifyingly; she strikes him:

> Queen. Don't glower at me—you are a fraud!
> Ha, ha, you are!
> A mere, smug, posturing fraud.

> Brandel (*in an agonized voice*). Don't!

> Queen. Ha! does it hurt? . . . Vanity! . . . Vanity!
> Mere mock-vanity, Brandel. You are not even angry!
> Oh you feeble mock-valiant fraud!

In her hysterical grief and her desire to justify herself, she becomes meanly dishonest (we are reminded of Edmund II's brutal treatment of the Bard). Suddenly, for a moment, Brandel grabs her by the throat.

Then—throughout the scene, the falling and rising emotions are convincingly portrayed—there is a sort of reconciliation: both are ashamed. As they stand a few feet apart, facing each other, the gulf between them becomes almost tangible—and of course the deep gulf has been there from the beginning of the play. Now, significantly and ironically, it is the Queen who invites and Brandel who will not move:

Queen   (*stretching her hand imploringly across* [the distance
          between them]). Oh, Brandel—try—for my sake—
          Reach your hand across . . . and I will hold you!

Brandel   (*not moving a muscle*). I cannot. There is no bridge
                now, not a rope or strand left . . .
          One cannot walk on air.

Queen.   No, Brandel?

Brandel. No. So I must go, Isabel . . .

It was Brandel who cut the ropes and fell. He has now made a
new assessment of that action; he quietly asks Isabel to forgive
him. But at this moment *she* sympathizes with *him*. In a sense
they both leap across the chasm:

Brandel. But forgive me one thing first.

Queen.   What? What, Brandel?—Anything!

Brandel. Isabel, I did not know how mad I was before . . .

Queen.   Mad?

Brandel. Or how cold-heartedly I tried to force you . . .

Queen.   Force me?

Brandel. . . . To be a thing like me . . .
          We believe or we don't.
          I thought that I could make you see.

Queen.   But I should have been . . . !

Brandel. A Queen? Should you?

They are getting to the bottom of themselves and of their conflict.
Brandel brings out his confession, placing his past before himself
and before Isabel, with passionate lucidity: "I tried to buy, with
sheer conviction as my cash,/What no man must,/Your conscience, Isabel." We can feel both his contempt for what was
bullying in his action and his humility as he realizes that it is

something very central in her—indeed it is Isabel herself—that he has tried to possess. At the same time, these lines have a formality and a finality which suggest the pattern of meaning and understanding that is being woven. At the next words one part of the pattern is completed:

Brandel. Then be free, be free, I beg you
Of guilt and misery on my behalf . . .
But try to see . . .

Queen. What?

Brandel. Why I did that.
I am . . . (*he pauses, looking for the word.*) . . . a
man . . .
A lost man . . .
But all men are lost, Isabel, in a way,
Because they cannot make a thing
That *really* lives—
Unless it is inside their heads . . . and that's only
half-alive.
Forgive me that then, if you can, and be done.

Queen. I accept and forgive you, Brandel.
What else could any poor woman do?
But please—accept me too.

Brandel. Of course.

Queen. I am a woman.

Brandel (*solemnly*). I accept that . . .

These lines illustrate well the complete simplicity (so much having gone before of course) with which Manson is able to tackle this profound conflict. In fact, the profundity of the conflict and its universality are brought out by the simple words: "men–lost"; "make," "lives"–"heads," "half-alive"; "poor women——do."

II *Characterization*

Isabel is a woman, rooted in actuality, in what she has felt. She has a real honesty, yet it is partly that fixed and unenterprising attachment to the facts of one's immediate condition, which can perhaps also be a sort of *dis*honesty. She is down-to-earth, a believer in ordinary *living*, frail: in one of her aspects she is a curiously modern figure. Brandel, on the other hand, it is quite possible to imagine as having flourished a full three hundred years ago (the suggestion I am bringing out is one which I think the play's time structure does contain): he is a hero, willing to limit his life, to cut it away, for something that he sees as noble; there is a touch of Don Quixote in him. He is, too, superbly masculine, in his virtues and in his faults. And of course he is a poet—the bard —astonished at the paradox that his work apparently leads him to deny the very values he is struggling for: his actions on behalf of *life* (as he conceives it) are not, it seems, themselves life-giving; what is imagined does not enrich but wars with reality. Brandel is even a priest, a celibate, trying to spread grace abroad, to change people spiritually by virtue of the sacrifice he performs.

Brandel is all these things:—man, hero, poet, priest. In him the richness of manliness is gathered. And yet he is a lost man: both his struggle with reality and his struggle with the woman who complements him and stands against him have failed. Brandel's despair and Isabel's despair, embodied as they are, affect us all. And perhaps they may affect *us*, his first readers and audiences, in a special way; for in the end, *The Festival* is a profoundly contemporary play. The antinomies which we confront in it are precisely those which are thrust with unusual force upon many sensitive people today. Is not a concern for normality and emotional security incompatible with any superimposed ideas or beliefs about "what a good life *should* be"—especially when these beliefs may sometimes call for a sacrifice of some part of one's living? Can concepts and duties be made fully and ordinarily human? Can one be both "responsible" and fully, *normally* alive? It is not unimportant that the great poet of our age, W. B. Yeats, has in the poem *Vacillation* dealt in his very different way with some of these "contraries":

> Although the summer sunlight gild
> Cloudy leafage of the sky,
> Or wintry moonlight sink the field
> In storm-scattered intricacy,
> I cannot look thereon,
> Responsibility so weighs me down.

Can the mind, with all its aspirations, and the body, with its rich demands, ever be one? And can a man and a woman ever really understand each other?

I have made these formulations of some of the themes that are thrown out by the emotional clash at the core of the play, not because the play ends or reaches its most important climax at this point, but because my fairly detailed analysis has gone on long enough. I shall deal with the second half of the play comparatively briefly. At the end of the scene I have been describing (Act II, Scene 1), we find that Brandel and Isabel have, by their generous acceptance of each other, placed themselves more firmly than ever in the benevolent grip of the trussed-up Bard. Now it is the Queen who encourages Brandel and describes what is happening:

> If his insight or sympathy and skill
> Like unsubstantial fingers
> Can strum across our throat chords still,
> After all these years,
> We may for once
> Speak with the clarity and courage of angels,
> And come together,
> And lie forever together in the dark—at rest.

The interchange between two ghosts which we have seen turns out to be only the prologue to what might almost be called the play proper. We are whirled back through time to the same scene three hundred years earlier.

III *Dialogue and Dynamics of the Play*

The Festival is never undramatic, and the dialogue is always human and "felt"; it is never merely polemical as the dialogue in Shaw or Sartre often is. But the play becomes more and more *physically* dramatic. We work our way toward Brandel's act itself; and as we move, the exact outline of the scene and the precise circumstances surrounding the breaking of the bridge become clear. And our involvement becomes at every moment fuller as the poet leads us back through the play's conflicting emotions on a spiral path which pierces deeper and deeper into these emotions and ever closer to the action which has both crystallized them and perpetuated them.

Yet at the same time, at the beginning of Act II, Scene 2, Brandel and Isabel *choose consciously* to go through everything again. They are willing to accept responsibility for what they have done. And they do not only (as in the previous scene) state clearly what their actions were; they live through them again. Thus they free themselves from remorse and anger and anxiety; what they did is given meaning, fitted into its pattern. They come to understand themselves and each other; strands of imaginative sympathy are thrown across the chasm between them; and, when in the next scene the bridge is finally broken and we see (or almost see) Brandel's actual fall, a spiritual bridge is there for the first time. The Bard's story, which is something real and before our eyes, enacts the very unifying which the festival proclaims. But there is nothing mechanical and simple about the solution, the "rest," which Brandel and Isabel achieve. They live out the important moments of their lives fully and accurately: the dance of exorcism contains all the sadness and bitterness of reality.

And so we move into the old story itself. We are plunged into the intensity of a summer day. We see Edmund and Isabel, vigorously alive, manacled together, fleeing from Edmund's inflamed subjects. It becomes clear that Isabel has been due to be crowned queen of the country across the ravine, but that—completely against the advice of her devoted first peer of the realm, Brandel —she has run away, and become the wife of Edmund, whom she despises. It is significant that Edmund has allowed some soldiers to fetter the two of them together and that he is afraid to cut off his arm in order to free himself from her, for she has become too exhausted to run any further. Yet, for all this, Edmund commands at least a pitying sympathy from the audience.

Brandel enters. He breaks the chain which joins them together (the action is symbolic) and says that he has come to take Isabel back. He is willing to take the cringing Edmund too. His demand is imperious, but he explains it by describing very vividly what has happened to their realm since she has left. At first there was the confusion of most of the ordinary people, and the despair of the old nobility, left powerless by the disappearance of the Queen. Then there was an insurrection and a time of chaos and near-madness. Now peace has been restored, and the nation desperately hopes that their Queen will return—and Brandel has promised them that she will. His sensitive and convincing account of these events makes us aware of the concrete reality of the human and political values that he is dedicated to, and his appeal to her is frank and moving.

And Isabel *is* moved, deeply; yet she cannot accept Brandel's deciding on her behalf, and she does not feel able to play the part that he has re-created for her. We are back at the central conflict. After a lively interchange, the man and the woman formulate their feelings with a new clarity and depth, in a passage of powerful poetry which is, unfortunately, too long to quote. But then at the very end of the scene Isabel does allow herself to be half convinced. She says grudgingly that she will return home with Brandel, and the three set off for the gorge.

Act II, Scene 3 is a scene of actions—actions crisply performed and actions cleanly described. It is in some ways like a scene from Hemingway, but the articulateness achieved in the previous scenes gives to the terse speeches of this scene a significance that Hemingway seldom manages to embody. We are on a rocky promontory just above Brandel's bridge (for it is he who has made it), and we see Brandel, Isabel, and Edmund in their crisis. They are being chased, and they find that there are soldiers on the bridge. Edmund is terrified and stupidly vicious; when Brandel and Isabel are forced to leave him (his ankle is broken) and make a dash for the bridge, instead of fighting as he had promised, he betrays them, ripping off his royal robes in order to do so. Isabel we see urgent and sensible and apparently ready to do what Brandel asks. Brandel's cutting and fall (described at the end of the scene by a group of soldiers) turns out to be even braver and more honorable—and more wasted—than we could have suspected: he dies not only that Isabel, who has got across the bridge, should be free to be a queen, but because he has solemnly promised not to outlive Edmund, whose final treachery he does not suspect.

It is the Festival of Death and Life; and the brief third act completes the relationship—the pattern of significances set up—between the dead people we have been seeing and the living people through whose mouths they spoke. We find ourselves back at the woodcutter's shack, in the early morning. The three main characters (the Bard, Isabel II, and Edmund II) are still asleep; but the others are discussing the mysterious enactment that has taken place during the night. The mean-minded Merchant puts forward the view that the King and Queen have simply experienced a nightmare bred of guilt; but the others believe that something real has happened and that the royal pair will wake up changed, having partly burned away their old selves just as Brandel and the first Isabel burned away their remorse.

When they wake up, they *are* changed—they are joyful, relieved, and repentant. The King frees the frozen Bard and asks for his forgiveness, and he and his wife stand in shame before the others. But to their surprise they are congratulated. The Bard has done his work well—the play, the ritual, and Brandel's part were his—but the King and Queen have played their parts fully and creatively too. Humbled by their guilts and doubts, they have opened themselves before reality, and imaginativeness has come upon them as a sort of grace. The King says: "The dead have been generous/And warned us, Isabel./I beat the Bard and burned his book,/Dead Edmund let him die on the bridge . . . / . . . it was myself I saw." Religious and moral awareness, it is clearly implied, grows from an ability and a willingness to imagine deeply.

And so the vision that has been engendered is seen as passing into everyday living (where it will have to be applied devotedly and strenuously, for the transformations we have witnessed are not miraculous) and into the festival itself. The play turns out at the end to be both a morality play and a comedy; and the festival is completed in dancing and boisterous fun (only the Merchant stands sourly by). But the final gaiety is a serious gaiety: it flows not only from a recognition of man's ability to grow in stature but also from an acceptance of life's mysterious processes and of the patterns that have been discerned in them.

CHAPTER 8

Captain Smith

M ANSON'S plays have a most deceptive simplicity of language—a simplicity which nevertheless completely conveys
to the attentive extremely complex thoughts and feelings. *Captain
Smith*, for example, is written largely in monosyllables; the language is simply constructed but charged with feeling. It is natural,
human, and unself-conscious, and it has the one indispensable
quality that art must have: it communicates the feeling—I will
not call it an illusion, for it is not exactly an illusion—that the
breath of life is in it.

I *Summary of the Action*

King Edmund I and Queen Isabel are hiding behind a fallen
tree from the pursuing revolutionary soldiers and their dogs; Edmund disappears to fetch water for the Queen, who is feverish
from exhaustion and heat. Suddenly and silently the revolutionary
Captain Smith enters unseen by her, slips a noose over her wrists,
and ties them to a branch over her head; when Edmund enters he
is immediately captured in a similar way. This beginning is full of
violent action and agonizing suspense, and the royal pair's struggle for life, supporting yet hating each other, is, naturally, rather
brutal: action and dialogue grip the attention from the first moment. It soon becomes very clear that the thick-set elderly Captain Smith is mad and also that he is an extremely kind and
humane man. Unfortunately, he is possessed by an unshakable
and insane series of convictions, the first of which is that God
hates madmen—therefore they are in hell and will be to all eternity unless they can be sane again. Secondly, he believes that he
can be cured of his madness if he can pay the huge fees (about
fifteen thousand pounds) of a doctor in a faraway country, and
that not to be cured would be an insult to God. He could get that
money (ten thousand pounds for the King, and five thousand for

the Queen, their "gazette price") if he handed them over alive to the revolutionary army, to be tortured and then killed. Thirdly, he thinks that their sufferings in such a case would be far less than a fleabite in comparison with being in hell for all eternity, his certain doom if he is not cured. Fourthly, he quite expects them to sympathize with him and understand that he is compelled, therefore, to hand them over. Captain Smith's madness and his lovable character are conveyed in almost every line.

At this point in the story, Brandel appears, walking through the forest on his way to his own adjoining country, with a bag of money (about ten thousand pounds in all, we learn later) which he needs to set that country free from usurpers who have overthrown the old nobility there and killed many of them, including all of his own family. Brandel and Captain Smith are old friends and companions in arms, for Brandel served for awhile in the Captain's army. "Gentle soul, what have you done?" he exclaims on seeing the captives, but when he tries to set them free, the Captain becomes terribly dangerous, drawing his heavy sword; Brandel is forced to desist. His dilemma is acute. He cannot bear to let the Captain sell the innocent King and Queen to torture and death, nor can he choose the only alternative, which is to kill his dear and good old friend, who is equally innocent.

Because of their complexity, compression, and essentially poetic quality, Manson's plays are extremely difficult to summarize. In the case of *Captain Smith*, it is impossible, for the course of the entire action proceeds from Captain Smith's madness, his lightning twists and turns of mood, always unexpected and irrational, but with a strange, insane logic (it is indisputably logic) in them. This causes the action to follow anything but an even course, nor can much idea of what happens be given without following all the fluctuations of the Captain's strange reasoning as revealed in the dialogue. I shall have to generalize, with an illustration or two, omitting all reference to the partly allegorical intent.

II *Act One*

Let us consider first what happens in the first of the three acts (each act is one scene long). Near the beginning of it Smithy is intent on handing over his royal captives in return for money to buy his cure, and Brandel's pleadings are in vain. But by the end of the act he has, with stupendous generosity, released the captives, sacrificing the possibility of a cure, he believes, and mortally offending God. Brandel is to help the King and Queen escape to his own country by climbing up a very steep mountain at night; Smithy, at the request of the Queen, who promises to look after him for the rest of his life, is to accompany them.

Before their release, the situation is fraught from moment to moment with the keenest suspense, because Captain Smith is *very* mad, because he has the two captives entirely at the mercy of his deftness, his strength, and his sharp sword, and because Brandel loves him and cannot bear to kill his excellent friend, though his doing so appears to be the only possible way of freeing the innocent captives. Mad reasoning is so absurd and unpredictable, the issues are so very serious, and we are made to feel so intensely for all four of the characters that the dialogue is often very comical and very painful at the same time, so that our reaction to it is sometimes a wild and startled laugh, accompanied by a sharp pang of pity and vicarious double-edged anxiety—pity for both sides, anxiety for both. Manson with his usual insight makes real to us all the aspects of this extraordinary situation.

We are made to feel acutely the mutual pressure of four personalities in a dangerous situation. The two royal personages, bound to each other by marriage and fate, are not very likable in their desperate struggle for life, until Captain Smith's generosity, by relieving them of its pressure, makes them able to feel less primitive emotions. Brandel, on the other hand, is a man of exceptional idealism, humanity, and courage. But the person who wins our deep affection and causes all the trouble is Captain Smith himself, an experienced soldier, courteous and tenderhearted, religious (in the broad sense) to the marrow of his bones. In fact, he is a saintly man, but a man stricken with madness and therefore terrible and highly dangerous. Almost his first words reveal something of these characteristics. When he first prevents the Queen from shouting for Edmund, "Your pursuers are mad," he says. "They think I'm mad." But: . . .

> . . . Don't move . . . ! Because
> I *am* mad, see? Ha! Ay, and cruel . . . as a mad wolf!
> See this sword? Oh, oh, it's heavy—ay, and sharp,
> (*He swishes it just over her head.*)
> One squeak and . . . sput!

I'll split you in two! Ha, ha, like a porker—
Spine and ribs on this side—spine and ribs on that—
Ha! Ha! Ha! Ha!

One can hear his tone in sound and rhythm. Could anything seem
more cruel than this lightning picture, with its hideously vivid
language, of what he may do, followed by the mad laugh? Then
comes a kind of childish game, equally mad, but suddenly gay,
when he dances around her for glee at his capture. When she
nearly faints with terror, he drops his sword and catches her.

There, there, there, never mind, never mind (*he says*)
Are you hurt . . . ? (*she shakes her head*)
No? Oh, no, no, no, no! Are you afraid? Of me? Poor Smithy?
There, there, wipe your pretty face . . . (*He takes out a hand-
    kerchief.*)
Smithy can see it's pretty . . . yes, even all dirty and tearful like
    this.
There, there, now smile at me.
(*tenderly*) Yes, you *are* pretty.

He means every word of his kindness; he treats her with real
affection and tenderness, almost as if she were a favorite child,
and yet it is crystal clear that at any moment he might suddenly
kill her. Captain Smith is a truly gentle soul; he is deeply
wounded if anybody suggests that he might hurt anyone; yet he
intends to hand these two over to certain torture and certain
death. The effect of this kind of thing is often upsettingly comic.
He is frightening because he is mad, and at the same time he is
charming and endearing because he is as innocent as a child.
When the King pleads with him not to hurt them, the Captain
"with a flash of maniacal fury" cries out: "Hurt! (*he slaps the
King's face*) Hurt you?" Then, realizing that he has done so, he
almost weeps with shame and contrition, but recovering himself—
"But still I did it suddenly, didn't I? Did I think?"—he says, relieved:

No! Nothing deliberate . . .
Surely it only stung? Didn't it?
(*He slaps himself resoundingly on the face.*)

> Ha! Just a little bit . . .
> Nothing. (*He beams.*)

That beam, so childlike and sweet-natured, has his insane logic in it. He himself is not cruel: that he is going to deliver them over to cruelty is the fault of his madness.

In a way, it is his profound religious faith that makes so kind a man even entertain the idea of selling two human beings for a reward. The others are all "as sane as sunlight," he explains, using an image that expresses feelingly how sad and dark his own life is. God looks at madmen with eyes that are "Opaque and milky like a blind man's eyes." This is an idea of such shuddering horror that Brandel cries out "Oh God have pity!" and Captain Smith explains that madmen do not deserve pity, for it was one of them who pricked God's eyes out.

Madness, Smithy explains, is a kind of agony of drabness, which may be (that is the horror of it) unending. And he yearns almost despairingly for a "shadow of light" or "play of light"—"On anything or through anything / A grass blade even . . . ! / Ha! just that! One light-lit blade would be—ah! heaven-lit! / Heaven-green— / Luminous and real alive." Suddenly, in speaking, he sees, to his immense delight, "a blade of grass glow green as emeralds . . ." and cloud-shapes "Building up snow-walls! Light-walls! Lovely!" The momentary respite makes him think how as a boy he thought the "flurries of storm wind / That tousled my downy hair / Were the fingers of God on his child." The image makes us think of him as still a guiltless child, as we feel indeed he is as he longs with an almost hopeless longing to be sane again.

Smithy's peculiar, mad logic leads to situations full of an excruciating irony. For example, the King, in his fear of death, realizes that he may be able to use the combination of unselfishness and insanity in the Captain to save himself, and he cunningly suggests that the best way out of the dilemma would be for Smith to kill himself. Smithy takes this suggestion quite seriously, and in spite of Brandel's horrified protests he is about to act on it: "Obliterate myself . . . ?" he says, pondering, "It might help." "It would help me," says the King, "and make no difference whatever to you." But as the King's hopes rise, suddenly Smithy remembers that the reward can buy him sanity, and it is his duty to God to be sane if he can. If he uses the reward to buy a cure, then "surely [God]

will love me again." Enraged, the King cries "You are mad!" "Of
course I am," rejoins the Captain:

> And so I must ask *you* to forgive me.
> I cannot die for you,
> And you, instead, must die for me—
> To bring me back to God.

> *King.* Grotesque beast! You're mocking me!
> You are not mad at all.

But he *is* mad, and he explains in some astonishment: "You will
only *die* for me." "If I could save *your* soul from Hell," he goes
on, with complete sincerity, "by simply dying, I would most willingly." And so the seesaw of wild suspense goes on until the King
demands of Brandel that he shall tell the truth. Can the ransom
money buy a cure for the Captain's madness? Brandel cannot bear
to dash Smithy's hopes and desperately suggests that the Queen
should answer. Some instinct warns Smithy: "But will she kill
hope, Brandel, with lies?" he falters. "She must not speak
then! / Despair's a great sin / And sweet hope must not bleed to
death." Cruelly the King retorts, "But false hope must!"

> *Captain (starting back as if struck).* That hurt me, Brandel!
>   Why? As if he thrust me through with some-
>   thing . . .

Brandel, regretting his own cowardice, tries to stop the Queen,
but it is too late. With a chilling spite she tells poor Smithy that
the few friends who told him he could be cured were lying.
Though shattered by this news, he forgives them: his "poor sick
disinherited friends" were only trying to win favor from the God
who hates him as a madman and therefore uses his friends to hurt
him. "Madam, I was his only friend," says Brandel, choking with
grief and fury, "And now he does not even have me!"

> *Captain.* Have you really deserted me, Brandel?
> *Brandel (overcome).* No, Smithy! Never!
> *Captain (touched).* Will you leave *God* for me?

Brandel (*hardly aware of what he is saying*). Willingly! Willingly!

Captain. God, that's courage!
(*proudly*) He is my friend, Madam—that sort! What
courage!

And in an impulse of almost supernatural generosity, he resolves
to free them.

The King and Queen are genuinely moved to gratitude, as
much as their shallow natures will allow. In reply to Smith's question about where will they go, the Queen replies with a kind of
petulant despair, "Does it matter?" Smithy, seizing her arm, cries
incredulously, "Matter? Doesn't it . . . matter? / I remain in hell
for you, / For ever and for ever in hell! (*He cries out*) Oh,
Brandel! / She doesn't even care!" "Smithy! Smithy!" cries Brandel,
"She does not mean it. She does not know— / Not even now!"

And the tenderhearted old man forgives her this terrible insen-
sitivity because "she is only young—and ignorant"; and with a
strangely touching gesture, he holds back her hair from her face
so that Brandel may see that "She is only a little girl . . . a
child / They must not catch her!" These fragments give far too
little idea of the continually surprising and moving quality of the
dialogue. It is fresh and natural, as always in Manson, and is
based on a belief in "the holiness of the heart's affections" and the
possibility of unselfishness and courage.

As the act ends, the four trudge off in perfect amity to begin
their difficult journey, Captain Smith carrying Brandel's posses-
sions. "I'm a mule," he says cheerfully, and Brandel responds jokingly, "A mad old army mule. . . ."

III *Act Two*

Most plays reach a climax, or turning point, near the middle of
the middle act. Events have been building up in a certain direction until then. At a certain point something happens that reverses
the direction, the tower of blocks begins to topple, by the last
scene it has completely fallen, and one arrives at the catastrophe
or denouement. This is not exactly what happens in *Captain
Smith*. In this play the action, because of Smithy's madness, constantly changes, without developing in any one direction until the
very end. Therefore in the middle act, Manson very wisely pro-

vides a breathing space, a delightful respite, where, for the space
of almost the whole act, Captain Smith is lucid, and therefore the
characters, and, at a remove, the audience, are freed from the
intense anxiety his madness causes them. Perhaps the climax
proper begins its slow turning in Captain Smith's soliloquy at the
end of the act.

The curtain goes up on a broad ledge traversing the bottom of a
towering cliff. There is a cave in the rock, and to one side a steep
and very narrow gully up which the four characters have to climb
to reach Brandel's country. The third act also takes place on this
ledge. And though the King is rather ill-tempered because of the
coming climb in the dark (they are all to sleep this day and climb
at night), the four characters are on not unfriendly terms. The
King has moments of anticipatory terror: "But it's sheer, man,
smooth as glass." "Not as bad as it looks," replies Brandel. The
Queen is frankly panic-stricken, and when Brandel and the Captain try to reassure her, Manson makes us feel both her femininity,
with a good deal of sweetness, dependence, and courage in it, and
also their essential kindliness, manly common sense, sensitivity,
and courage. In addition, he gives, with his usual lively immediacy, the strongest sense of what it is like to make a climb up such
a rock face. The terrified Queen is not easily reassured: "No! I'd
rather die than even try such a thing at all." "Isabel, these moments pass," says Brandel:

> The night will pass—day will come
> And you will be sitting in the sun on top—
> Looking down;
> We will all be up—looking down, laughing,
> Smithy will take his first pipe of the day,
> And you will say:
> "Well, that was nothing, was it?"—half lying—
> But it will also be half true.

Earlier, Brandel has described to the Queen, in a graphic passage of fresh, natural, descriptive poetry of the kind of which
Manson is a master—a passage beginning "It'll all be over in one
night, Isabel"—how next morning the mist they are in now will be
gone; they will look down at sunup from the top of this cliff, from
his own very different but still lovely high country, upon hers lying far below like the map of another world.

These two vignettes make us feel something of the sweet peace and comfort the words must drop into the Queen's breast; the fugitives rest and drink cold water from the cave; these details, together with the words, create a strong sense of a heaven of peace to come, which the climbers will certainly attain to when they have got to the top. All this serves the essential purpose of providing for the audience a much-needed respite from the intense emotional strain of the play. This sense of relief, we find in due course, is cruelly ironic.

The King, Queen, and Brandel then go into the cave to sleep. But Smithy has flouted God's mercy and has brought eternal hell down upon himself. He knows that he will not be able to sleep, and, speaking aloud, he tries to calm himself: "Poor old Mulligan [his alcoholic friend] knows it—the terror of it / Fears them—the long nights Things talk to him in the dark . . . / What things? God knows." His own terror is growing as he thinks of it, and it reaches a climax of horror in that almost hysterical "God knows." What form will Hell take now?

> . . . Steady!
> Steady, steady, Smithy . . .
> Sit quite steady on a rock and smoke. (*He sits down.*)
> That'll fool him!
> How could a man sit quite still smoking
> If he were afraid of anything, eh . . . ? (*He tries to smoke.*)
> Your hand is shaking, Smithy! You're afraid?
> Of what?

But he cannot even smoke! His childish ruse for deceiving God has failed him, for a nameless dread makes his hand shake so that he cannot even hold the comforting pipe. He walks up and down and looks up at the cliff above him, but it is so misty that he cannot even see how bright the sun must be there. To distract his mind, he tries to think of the climb: experienced climber as he is, he will be able to climb up to the sunny top; perhaps he will be able to climb up out of his terror:

> When you were a little boy, remember?
> You could find finger- and toe-holds anywhere,
> Would carefully scratch away lichen from the rock,
> Fit a finger-tip into a crack that no-one else could see

And pull up—step up on your toe—
Oh, so easily!
There are always *some* cracks somewhere
On any cliff face, however smooth . . .

But suddenly a hideous idea comes into his mind:

Unless—yes, but he could
Obliterate every trace of them—
Make every foothold of your mind
As smooth and sliding-down as glass . . . !

There is an extraordinary power in this image of the hopeless and
desolate confusion of madness. For the mind not to be able to
hold on to anything, to grip anywhere, for it always to slip, and
slip!

But there is yet worse, unimaginable as it is to sane men, for
Smithy to endure. As he thinks of this continuous sliding down,
with not the slightest crack for fingerhold or toehold to grip by, he
calls out in shuddering horror: "And it's idle—idle!—to think you
will fall . . . / Where to? / Is there a bottom?" What an image of
eternity is presented in these simple words. Milton's phrase "bottomless perdition" assumes a different reality for us from that he
gives it and in this different way becomes almost real to us—for
the single moment beyond which we cannot endure to face it. I
think that by the details of this climbing image Manson makes it
perhaps even more real to us than Lawrence does in his poem
Abysmal Immortality. And the play being emphatically a poetic
unity, the image is dependent upon, and has been made all the
more eloquent by, the whole of the previous discussion among the
four characters of the coming climb.

In an intolerable restlessness, Smithy walks to the edge of the
drop and looks down: "Mist . . . mist . . ." he comments, in extreme depression. "As white and smothering-blind down there /
As it is all round me—or above. / That's your world, Smithy!
All in a mist. And no way up." The image makes us feel keenly
the awful, never-to-be-ended suspense of his life, now that the
hope of a cure has been taken away again. But the old man, with
heartbreaking courage, tries to rally himself:

Well, what then? Weep? Will it help?
Smithy, Smithy! God held out his hand to cure you . . .
And you . . . ?
Oh, God, give me a crack or finger-hold
There on the glass face of my brain—
Just one grip on it!
And everything down there will be clear,
The air light,
The fields and valleys bright,
Green, golden,
Even the dun, fallow lands would be lovely,
The sky blue,
And I could sleep too,
Like the rest.

The poetry is clear, lucid, intense: we are made to enter into and to pity deeply the old madman's vision of the bliss it would be to be sane again, if only for a moment. But the vision does not last: "But God hates you, Smithy!" he goes on. "What's there to do then . . . do then . . . do then . . . ? / Listen to the echo!" How utterly desolate the echo of his own words echoing the empty echo from the mountain sounds in this context. It implies that there is nothing anywhere to be done. "Go with these folk?" he asks himself. "Where / Where then? Go home? / To what?" And suddenly his worst fear of all, or rather his worst immediate fear, of claustrophobia, rises intolerably in his breast: "They'll lock you up anywhere / Here or there . . . / Whatever you say or do / Wherever you go." And he falls on his knees in despairing terror. We cannot but pity him with all our force. We are to discover in the next act why Smithy is afraid of being locked up and why the idea of being locked up (as the lines just quoted reveal) is unbearable to him.

IV *Act Three*

From the soliloquy at the end of Act Two it is clear to us that the respite we have all enjoyed (and even Smithy has enjoyed it at first while absorbed in tramping and climbing) is not likely to last much longer. It is the King, with his rather disagreeable, shallow character, who finally inadvertently destroys it. The next act opens on the ledge in sunlight, early in the afternoon; the sleepers are awake and mean to begin the climb soon. But Smithy is brooding gloomily. The King, who has not an inkling of what Smithy has sacrificed for him, taunts him with being as much afraid of the coming climb as he is, and Smithy is stung. He begins to throw things about out of his knapsack until at last he finds what he is looking for, a medal inscribed "For Bravery." Between Smithy and Brandel, at the insistent demand of the King and Queen, the story of how the medal was won emerges: it appears that Smithy, once falsely accused of treachery, was locked up and beaten daily in a lunatic asylum for years because he would not confess. After ten years, Smithy, now extremely confused, decided that he must be guilty, confessed, and was completely forgiven. Then the man who had accused him died after confessing that he, not Smithy, had been the traitor. This horrifying story moves the King and Queen strongly, but Brandel suddenly realizes that recalling it has excited Captain Smith too much, and in a second we are back where we began: Captain Smith has leapt at the Queen, grabbed her around the neck, and has pointed his dagger at her throat; threatening to kill her if he is not implicitly obeyed, he commands Brandel to tie up the King. Smithy can no longer bear the thought of being locked up again.

The seesaw of Act I starts again. Brandel buys the Queen's freedom from Smithy with half the money meant to help free his country, but she refuses to go. He has only half the King's price left, so he cannot buy *his* freedom. The Queen then persuades Brandel that the only way out is to kill Smithy, and she creates an opportunity. When it comes to the point, however, Brandel cannot do it, and shouting "No!" in horror, he covers his face with his hands. Smithy turns around, sees what has happened, and in grief and despair, throws his sword at the Queen's feet, crying, "Quick, Queen, despatch me!" But Brandel snatches the sword out of her grasp and throws it away in horror and revulsion. Nor does he prevent Captain Smith from scrambling for it and getting it back. The Queen falls on her knees and begins to pray silently.

At this point, a faintly possible solution occurs to the quixotic Brandel. He offers the Captain his remaining five thousand pounds in return for a chance to fight him for the King's freedom, Brandel fighting with his bare hands, Smithy with his heavy sword. Smithy, of course, hesitates: "Are you afraid of me?" taunts Brandel. "Silly, silly boy!" replies the Captain, "I am sad suddenly / Look what my madness has led you into." The King, though ashamed, urges Brandel on. "There's *some* chance," he pleads. The Queen cannot bring herself to dissuade him. "Do not let them distress you, Brandel," says Captain Smith. "Can't you see they are not like you or me? / I cannot be in hell for eternity, / You cannot be deliberately less of a man / Than you know you can be." The essence of quality and spiritual heroism is in those last succinct two lines. "We are fortunate, aren't we," replies Brandel ironically, and the Captain replies in all seriousness, "Yes, we are fortunate."

Captain Smith takes it that this fight is God's answer to the Queen's prayer: it is to be a fight between "God's man," who is obviously Brandel, and "the devil's man"—himself, being mad, and therefore God's enemy. So his mad logic tells him, but he loves God, and he loves Brandel, and at the last moment a kind of noble cunning in his madness—a cunning that springs from his central warmth and purity of heart and his colossal courage—takes over, and he cheats himself in Brandel's favor. He pretends to have become suddenly cruel and corrupt, slapping the King's face. "Well, come then, I'm waiting . . ." he cries, "You'd better win, boy." "I will," says Brandel. "Ay, better win" taunts the Captain "they're both mine again!"

> To sell! Fifteen thousand! Ha! Ha! Ha!
> And your cash too. Dear me, you're dumb, boy!
> But I will be sane—and rich as well!

As that does not yet make Brandel attack him, he goes further: he spits on Brandel, who remains impassive; then he leaps toward the Queen, brandishing his sword before her face: "How will a hack or wipe across her face with this / Improve her, Brandel?" "Don't," shouts Brandel, but still he does not fight; the Queen calls Smithy "Coward!" And he, smiling bitterly, says "Am I? Catch, Brandel!" and throws his sword at Brandel, who catches it instinctively; and as Captain Smith jumps at him, a second later, Brandel runs him through quite by instinct.

The shock is electrifying. Captain Smith stands for a moment, impaled, and puts his arms around his dear friend, crying "Comfort me!" but Brandel cannot move. Then Smithy pulls himself off the sword and falls. Brandel rushes to help him, but it is too late, and as the Captain dies, he calls out, "Down—down—and God can't see!" "No!" moans Brandel. "Everlastingly down! Into the dark" cries the Captain. "It opens up!—All hell!" His last words, as he raises himself slightly, are: "King, Madam, see, I *am* brave" and again, despairingly, he cries "Down!" as he dies.

This death of brave Captain Smith is profoundly moving. The audience has been made to feel the charm and beauty of his affectionate character and the sadness of his insanity, but here the beauty and the sadness meet in a focus of extreme concentration. The whole play is, as it were, distilled into this ending. The dream of the peace and happiness (built up by the poetry of the second act) that the characters would have enjoyed if they had climbed to the top of the cliff is negated here. Captain Smith was fated never to go up but to die imagining that he was doomed to slide forever down "the glass face of [his] brain."

Brandel is dumb with grief and self-reproach and goes blindly off stage. The King and Queen have been freed. She runs after Brandel. The King, ignoring everything else, bends over Smithy's body and composes his limbs, uttering the following grateful words of almost heartbroken admiration and contrition:

King. Rest in peace, Smithy.
You are home at last.
Does it surprise you opening your eyes
That all the company of paradise
Welcomes you like an old friend?
I could see you died for me.
Ask God to send me compassion too.
Do you hear what I dare ask of you, Smithy . . . ?
For my mind now is in the dark, as yours was,
And I cannot see my way at all.

Then he covers Smithy with his cloak. This prayer is uttered by a man who once said to Smithy, "God is a fraud." His mind is now in the dark, but he does believe in one thing: he has experienced through Smithy a spirit of goodness in the universe. The Queen comes back weeping, and is bitter and sharp.

Brandel (with whom she is more than half in love), has not even seen her, and this fact and her words about it convey, with penetrating poetic terseness Brandel's extreme grief, his everlasting regret, his sense of the Captain's unutterable value, his deep imaginative understanding of what his sacrifice cost poor Smithy, and his horror at the fact that it was he himself who killed him, feelings too overpowering to make anything else—the King, the Queen, Smithy's body lying exposed, the future, *anything*—have any meaning for him whatever for the time being. "Well, what now, Edmund?" says the Queen (*with desperate levity*). And they decide to climb up to the top of the cliff. Once there they will part, but meanwhile, "We will tie ourselves together again," they say. On this symbolic note, bitter but resigned, Manson's history of the King and Queen closes, and the play ends.

CHAPTER 9

The Magnolia Tree

*T*HE *Magnolia Tree* was produced in 1966 by the Royal Lyceum Theatre, Edinburgh. It has been reprinted entirely in the international theatre magazine, *Gambit,* and has been produced, in a radio version, by the South African Broadcasting Company. The main idea for the play is taken from a short story called "Kesa and Morito" by the Japanese writer Akutagawa; two Japanese films, *Roshomon* and *The Gates of Hell,* which had greatly impressed Manson by their poetic and dramatic power and economy, are founded on it. The story is poor; the murder in it of a man the murderer did not hate for a woman he did not love, is almost entirely unmotivated; Manson became fascinated with the problem of what could cause such an act and how he could make it credible. The result was a play in three acts, *The Magnolia Tree.*

I *Action of the Play*

The play has, strictly speaking, only three characters, and in every scene except the last, only one, for everything that occurs on the stage, except in that last scene, happens in the mind of an old blind priest of eighty, an Abbot named Morito; in the last scene only his two contemporaries and lifelong friends, Kurodo and Kawachi, also appear in the flesh. The first scene opens with the Abbot standing under a magnolia tree in a Japanese garden. In the background is the deserted house of Wataru Saemon, with a window conspicuously placed on one wall. It emerges from the opening soliloquy that the Abbot murdered someone fifty years ago, that on every anniversary of the murder he has come to this spot to do penance by recalling it, and that he has come here now for what he believes will be the last time, to go through in his mind with the most ruthless honesty he can summon exactly how

136

the murder came about. He wishes by a huge imaginative effort to understand fully at last exactly why it happened.

In order to do this he remembers himself at about thirty, the age at which he committed the murder; and again, as his mind goes back further into the past, at the age of twenty-five; then at thirty again; and so on. He remembers his past selves so vividly that they actually appear on the stage, with the result that four actors are needed to play the part of Morito—the real Morito at eighty, now an abbot; himself at thirty, at that time a Samurai; at twenty-five; and in two scenes, an Actor-Morito, who is watched by the Abbot-Morito and the Samurai-Morito conversing together. Other visionary figures are Kesa, and except in the last scene, where they are real, Kurodo and Kawachi. When the Actor-Morito and Kesa are together on the stage, they mime the actions which the watching Morito-at-thirty is describing to the Abbot, and every now and again their usually unheard words become audible. The effect of this is dramatic in the extreme, for by this device the spoken words strike upon the ear of the audience with a special weight. Another extremely effective dramatic device is that at certain points in the story the watching Abbot cries out suddenly to the Morito who is describing what happens, "Don't tell me any more." This suggests with the utmost sharpness how unbearably ashamed he still is at eighty of what he did at thirty.

This technique of the four Moritos is skillfully used to reconstruct the past life, and especially the inner life, of the four people in the play, but Morito's and Kesa's especially. The flashbacks, interspersed with comments from the Abbot and the visionary Samurai, looking back (as it were) on various episodes of the past, work very much as memory does a long time after the events. The comments of the Abbot and the Samurai represent, as it were, the generalizations that memory makes about what has happened, whereas the flashbacks are like those astonishingly vivid patches of recall we often have when we remember exactly what everything looked like and the very words that people uttered, however long ago. The technique also helps to create the compelling aura which surrounds this play: the growing sense we have, all the time we are watching it, of a deep and difficult truth being slowly conjured up out of the dark backward and abysm of time and finally out of the very grave. Inside this aura is the flesh-

and-blood story in which a sort of creative suspense is kept alive
by a myriad touches in the texture of the writing.

The story that is slowly revealed in the first two acts goes as
follows: Three young Japanese men of about twenty-five, Morito,
Kurodo, and Kawachi, are great friends, but Morito is something
of a mystery to Kurodo and Kawachi. They are clever, witty, goodhearted young men who take life lightly, and when *they* are gaily
and enthusiastically in love, without being very serious about it,
Morito is deeply troubled, though he is "happy, as one is." He is in
love with Kesa, and what troubles him is that he suspects his love
of being lust. Also, he is obsessed with a desire for heroic achievement, and so he becomes a soldier, while Kurodo and Kawachi go
into the Civil Service.

Five years later Morito, as a Samurai, comes back from the
wars, still sick with his passion for Kesa, who meanwhile has married an important civil servant, Wataru Saemon. Morito, though
no longer in love with her, is consumed with a passionate regret
that he has never possessed her body. One day when he is alone
with her in her aunt's house, "Knowing that she would misunderstand me / I seized her roughly / Had my way with her / Shamed
her body and destroyed my soul."

Then he acts strangely, impelled by a mixture of emotions:
shame, contrition, brief vindictive hatred of Kesa, because unconsciously he fears his guilt ties him to her forever, pity for her
because she loves him, and rage at himself for daring to pity
her. This makes him, on a strong, false impulse, assure her that he
loves her; to make his lying words sound true to them both, he
swears that he will kill Wataru Saemon for her. Then, as Kesa
demurs, but he knows she is listening, and is angry with her for it,
he goes on repeating "soft endearments / From my [his] empty
heart," telling her over and over again that he loves her, though he
does not.

There is an interval of darkness on the stage; a period of love-
making presumably intervenes. When the lights go up again, it
becomes clear that this has had a curiously hardening effect on
Morito: he despises himself because he almost hates Kesa while
swearing that he loves her. She knows this more clearly than ever;
yet when he repeats his offer, she replies: "Yes, Morito, you must
kill Wataru." For as long as he wants her, however unlovingly, she
cares for nothing else. Her consent adds to his guilt toward her,

for now he has committed her to accepting a monstrous thing.

But he cannot face the thought of murder, and to escape from it he rushes out into the streets and gets extremely drunk. In this condition, chance leads him to the pleasure house where Kurodo and Kawachi have dined together and are now just "delicately poised between drunkenness and sobriety." In his maudlin state, Morito imagines that they are unhappy too, and to stop his drunken insistence they pretend that they *are* unhappy. They are unhappy, they say, vying with each other in making up a dramatic story, on behalf of their poor friend, Wataru Saemon, a man of exquisite taste, because he is humiliated by being linked to an ugly, clumsy, tongue-tied wife. Since they have never seen Kesa themselves and have no idea that Morito even knows her, they are obviously enlarging on Wataru's disloyal criticisms. Their account of Kesa strikes a blow at the most sensitive core of Morito's conscience, and also at something in his attitude to Kesa that *is* a kind of love, for he has a very strong sense of her value as a human being. She is *not* ugly, he cries passionately: "You are ugly! We three are ugly. / Ugly! Ugly!—inside our souls! / All men are monsters! Monsters! . . ." and when Kurodo and Kawachi leave, still in utter ignorance of the enormous crisis that is taking place in Morito, the soldier Morito is weeping.

As a result of this encounter, and "perhaps because I *was* a soldier," Morito goes back to Kesa at daybreak. He finds her still lying on the floor, as he had left her the night before, in utter despair; and the courage with which she takes the honest admission she then wrings from him that he does not love her makes him mistake the emotions that overwhelm him (in which compassion predominates) for love. What he says, however, is "Kesa, this must end," and she is about to faint with misery when he catches her in his arms; feeling again the softness and familiarity of her body, and changing what perhaps he meant to say, he cries: ". . . It must end! He must die, / And I will kill him for you, Kesa! / I will kill Wataru Saemon. I swear." "Yes, kill him, kill him, kill him, Morito!" sobs Kesa frantically, and they cling to each other passionately.

Thus far the first two acts. It is clear, even from this rough summary, that Morito's motive for the projected murder is to comfort somehow the woman to whose love he cannot fully respond, a woman whom he had, in effect, mortally hurt by dishonestly using her body without loving her, and toward whom he feels miserably guilty because her unhappiness is largely his fault —though it is not wholly so, for he would love her if he could. As a result of this he feels from the very center of his being that she may demand of him anything she will. She, for her part, has too passionate and desperate a need for whatever comfort he can give her to be able to refuse what he offers, even though it involves him in murder.

These are the bones of the first two acts. Manson has accepted the challenge thrown down by Akutagawa's story, and it is clear even from these bones that he has convincingly motivated the idea behind it. But the full motivation of the theme can only be grasped by reading in its entirety the play itself—a most beautiful, powerful play, very rich and strange in texture, strange and haunting in the "atmosphere" that texture creates. The living breath of the play, like that of all poetry, resides in the texture and in the construction.

Of that texture I can give only a few examples. The tragedy begins with the words, spoken by the Abbot as he stands under the magnolia tree, looking toward the window of the deserted house: "Is there anyone there," he says, "listening behind that window?" He goes on, "Who am I talking to if not to you?" and he tells that he comes here every year "To talk to you / Though it is fifty years ago to-night I killed you."

This window in the background has throughout the play a dramatically and poetically effective role in creating suspense. The house is Wataru Saemon's, in which the murder was committed, the window the one in which fifty years ago Kesa placed a lamp as a signal to the watching Morito to come in and do the deed. The old Abbot therefore looks toward it with a peculiar intensity of remembrance, and when the visionary Samurai first appears, he is pacing up and down restlessly, watching the window and waiting with feverish anxiety for the light to appear. The blind old Abbot asks if the moon is coming up, for he is aware of something bright:

   Morito (*starting*). The moon! I'd forgotten! Climbing up and up!
             And the world rolling round and away
             To another day . . .
             (*He starts.*) What is that moaning?

"The wind in the trees . . ." replies the Abbot, but the Samurai is so strung up that he imagines something sinister is touching him; then, calming himself, he realizes that it was only a leaf: "The night is full of dead leaves—like locusts— / Thousands of them rustling down!" The remembering Abbot is almost as desperately nervous in retrospect as is the Samurai who still has to do the deed: two kinds of memory are mingling, the slightly less vivid generalizing one, and the intensely vivid re-creating one. In this passage a variety of details—the Abbot's blindness; the hint of something ominous about the moonlight that makes both Abbot and Samurai think with dread and horror of the lamp that will soon be shining in the window; the hint of coming destruction in the locust image (the suggestion that the multitudes of leaves "rustling down" are like those locusts that wantonly devastate whole fields of wheat); the idea of pain in the moaning of the wind; and, in the lines about the moon climbing up and up, "And the world rolling round and away/To another day," the suggestion that what will so soon be done will be forever as irrevocable as the days that vanish with the rolling world—all these details are fused by the poetry to create a feeling of immense sadness and ill-omen.

Next let me quote one or two of the many passages which illuminate the complex nature of Morito's feeling for Kesa: he explains that when he met her it was as if he had suddenly fallen sick of a "terrible shaking fever"; and when, in a very gay, amusing and poetic scene (Act I, Scene 2), the youthful Kurodo and Kawachi tease their "poor, sad, very pure, noble, love-sick friend," they say jokingly, "his love eats him inside . . . like a worm / Poor devil!"

> Kawachi (*impudently*). Are you telling me, Kurodo,
> That he's never felt her thigh?
>
> Kurodo. I am telling you, Kawachi,
> That he's never heard her sigh.
>
> Kawachi. Has he never kissed her nipples?
>
> Kurodo. Never, Never kissed her nipples,
> Never even stroked her hair!

This is true at the time. Morito never is to sleep with her in love, and the effect upon him five years later when he seizes her

roughly in the deserted house and has his "way with her," is, at
first, revulsion. On that hot afternoon she appears repulsive: "The
shuttered sunlight struck the floor," he says, "Lit up the dusty air
in slats / Slashed her kimono in dark and light strips And cut her
face in three. / She was ugly." "Was she truly so?" enquires the
Abbot gently, for fifty years later Morito is not sure whether it
was only that he and Wataru had made her feel so.

> *Morito.* I said she was ugly
> And her face thick-coated with dead-white powder
> Had lost what bloom and charm
> I might have seen there five years ago
> Her hair hung lank, a little dirty.
> Dark rings made her eyes look sad.
> Her teeth, I saw, protruded, and one in front was
>   chipped.

Yet "the blood in me roared like a river."

The description in simple word and detail is not only brilliantly
vivid but utterly ruthless in its remembered cold objectivity. For
even in the heat of his obsessive desire, his heart is cold. Only the
touch about her eyes looking sad reveals a compassion that the
ensuing conversation deepens. It is clear from this that Kesa's
marriage is a failure and that she is pathetically lying when she
tells Morito how happy she is and how delicately her husband
expresses his affection for her. The rough carnal embrace to which
Morito then subjects her is the result of a complex mingling of
pity and loathing of himself for daring in his own "foulness" to
pity her; of illogical anger with her for being trivial enough to lie
about Wataru's affection when all the time she knows, and he
knows that she knows, that *he* has loved her with a much deeper
though silent kind of love; and finally of the obsessive desire to
achieve her. But the effect of it is even greater revulsion. When
she rises, he finds her so ugly "that I half raised my hand to strike
her back to the floor." It might have been better if he *had*, he says,
for when instead he uttered lying words of love, he sensed that he
had stepped on ground "That slid as an avalanche from under
me."

All this complexity of feeling in a strange and unusual character
—a most honest, sensitive, and serious character—is expressed

with astonishing force and clarity in vivid natural words, simple natural sentences, and simple natural speech rhythms. Manson is right to seek power in the natural language of people capable of "own-thinking" and "own-feeling," of feelings and thoughts deep and delicate and senses alive and alert, instead of in the debauched idiom full of shocking but meaningless obscenities of an age that seems to mistake verbal violence and vulgar crudity for strength.

In another passage there is an elaborate sea image that the watching Samurai uses to help explain part of what happened when, on returning at daybreak to Kesa after his night of confused and drunken misery and guilt, he finally resolved for certain to kill Wataru Saemon. When he returned to find her still lying on the floor in despair, Kesa got up with the red sunrise that shone through the shutter's chink glowing "sugar-pink on her cheek-bone a second / As if she were an actress." I could see, he says, "That her beauty was still lost to me / And was suddenly sad." In her honest desire not to bind the man she so truly loves, she begs him with the utmost sincerity not to pretend that he loves her but to admit it if he only "dully and brutally" desires her and loathes her while he does so. And the Actor-Morito, compelled by her sincerity, admits it. And at first she says "You're free. Be free of guilt towards me too—and go." On the inner stage this part of the play has been acted by Kesa and the Actor-Morito. Now the watching Samurai takes over the story. Kesa has accepted the admission bravely but has begged the Actor-Morito, "Tell me that my mind is not ugly." At this point, feeling "no evil in himself as he speaks," comments the watching Samurai, Morito says "what his heart must say." Such an ocean swell of pity, tenderness, gratitude, and relief overtakes him,

> That the frail ship of my good sense floundered
> And what before I knew was lust
> I thought to be turned to melting trust,
> Compassion and understanding.

There is no room to quote the whole of this powerful image, every part of which works to express the complex emotions that overwhelm the Samurai. He concludes: "Yet it wasn't pity / That made me say what I did say in the end." What he did say is enacted by the Actor-Morito and Kesa on the inner stage. It is,

first, "Kesa, this must end"; and finally, after her half-faint of misery, "It must end! He must die, And I will kill him for you,
Kesa / I will kill Wataru Saemon. I swear!"

It is in the very complexity and irrationality, in the shifts and
changes in all this, that the truth resides. Morito's indignation
against Wataru, after the wineshop incident, is at its height. The
sight of Kesa lying in such anguish on the floor, the pathetic sugar-
pink on her cheeks, which yet cannot make her beautiful again in
his eyes, his longing to find her beautiful and love her again, her
courage and illusionless straightness, his gratitude to her for it—
all help to overwhelm him, and his mind is flooded, most dangerously, as the sea image suggests, with the illusion, helped by
memory of past love, that it is love, not lust or pity, that floods
through him. The poetry expresses with lucidity, subtlety, and
power both Morito's desperate fight for self-knowledge at the
fateful moment and the generosity and unselfishness of the nature
that is defeated in that fight.

Yet even then he keeps his head. Kesa cannot bring herself to
watch his face as he speaks. Instead she will listen, she promises:
"I will listen for everything / That lips, teeth and tongue can
tell. / I will attend like a little mouse / Even to your breathing."
This eloquently expresses how certainly she knows that he means
to tell her the truth, and what the truth is; the mouse image conveys her frightened and extreme intensity, and the speech has a
piercing sadness. And he does mean to tell her the truth, for in the
words he finally does say, "Kesa, this must end!," his real meaning
—that they must not meet again—has jumped out of him "like a
tiger," says the watching Morito; and he knows he has wounded
Kesa by it as much as if he had stabbed her through the heart. He
almost expects to see the blood come spreading from the wound,
and she begins to fall forward in a faint. Then, in spite of all his
attempted honesty and control, he is defeated—defeated by physical contact—the familiar feel of her body as he grabs her around
the hips. That touch makes her too real. He no longer cares for
honesty, nor does she; they cannot in their agonized, passionate
need, feel anything at all but the need to have it proved by an act
as extreme as murder that what they know to be false is true. Kesa
is not even thinking of the fact and consequences of murder. All
she can feel at the moment, and everything she is is absorbed in
feeling it, is hysterical relief and thankfulness that the tension is

broken and that the words she so feared have not been and will not be spoken. And when Morito says again, "It must end!" and then changes what he meant to say, and cries, "It must end! He must die, And I will kill him for you, Kesa!," she replies, sobbing frantically "Yes, kill him, kill him, kill him Morito!"

People who do not understand passion, and the basic need for truth, will never understand Manson. Morito becomes a murderer because he is loyal: all he cares about now is to give the girl he has injured some kind of convincing proof of his loyalty. For Morito believes in loyalty. In Act I, Scene 3, the Abbot says that despite the boredom and the slow erosion and corruption of the soul in military life, a soldier "Must bring out alive within a dead breast / Those dreams that filled his young heart with fire." The Samurai answers: "Father, I am faithful too. / . . . All my acts, as facts, I have been / And still am, / And will be, bound to, / Up to, through and beyond / The gates of hell," for soldiers recognize "The necessity and the blind stupidity / Of faithfulness unto death." The necessity and blind stupidity, two equal factors, are what carry him to the very act of murder.

The third act brings a tremendous surprise. In the first soliloquy, the one spoken by the Abbot at the beginning of the play, Morito is addressing, but never by name, the person whose head he struck off for Kesa's sake fifty years ago. Throughout the first two acts we have assumed that the victim was Wataru Saemon. Now the old man speaks a second soliloquy at the beginning of the third act. He is alone. The Samurai has disappeared. The Abbot has, in fact, fully re-created in memory the steps leading to the murder and so has discovered his own motives for it. "And what is left to act out but the killing? / Oh God! Spare me the horror and terror and shame of that again!" And he tells how, when the lamp did finally flare in the window, and he went in with his drawn sword and struck, he saw not Wataru's but Kesa's head roll away from him. This information comes to the audience with an almost electric shock.

Then he earnestly prays to Kesa's spirit to come to him in a dream and make him understand what made her substitute herself for Wataru that night. When the curtain goes up again we are in Kesa's bedroom, with a large shuttered window, a bed, Japanese fashion, on the floor, and a small lamp burning very low on a table in the middle of the room. Kesa enters, "agitatedly walking to and fro." She is so distracted that when the Abbot addresses her, she takes him for a ghost and talks freely to him as a being who (being dead) cannot stop what she is going to do. (The reverse is true, of course—she is dead and he is alive.) Soon her intention becomes clear. Wataru, by her management, is asleep in a different room. She means to unshutter the window and put the lamp there, and when Morito comes in to kill Wataru Saemon, Kesa will be in the bed, and he will strike off her head instead of her husband's. The Abbot is powerless to prevent this, because of course it has already happened.

Kesa's mood is one of desolate sadness, with not an atom of vindictiveness in it toward anyone, either Wataru or Morito. A profound sadness permeates the entire scene.

Kesa   (*terrified when the Abbot offers to turn up the lamp*).
        No! Leave it! Leave it! Don't touch it!
        I'm not ready yet.
        There's so much to set at rest
        And rock asleep within my breast.
        Why are the doors and shutters clattering—
        Banging and banging—
        What is it?

Abbot. The wind. A sudden wind's sprung up.
        A cold wind, Kesa. . . .
        The winter's coming.

Kesa.   It's death.

Abbot. Listen.

Kesa.   Is it rain?

Abbot. Wind in the pine trees. Sighing like the sea.

Kesa   (*listening intently*). . . . Or rain at sea—far out in a
            little boat—
        Exactly like a rain-squall
        Hissing through the dark towards you
        Across the heaving silent sea.
        (*There is no noise but suddenly she tenses and speaks
            almost hysterically.*)
        Why is everything banging, clattering,

> The whole house shifting and tearing
> As if it were made of mere parchment or paper?
> Close them, silence them,
> Shut the house still!

Abbot. It will not wake your husband, Kesa.

It is difficult to say quite why this passage is so compelling. How human the feelings are; how simple the words! Yet the combined words and the rhythms they fall into have a powerful and varied vitality in them. They express and combine two kinds of life: on the one hand, that going on outside among the pine trees, on the sea, and in the house; on the other, what is happening in Kesa's bosom. The terror Kesa has of turning up the lamp too soon is feelingly shown in the strong, alarmed rhythms of "No! Leave it! Leave it! Don't touch it! / I'm not ready yet." She cannot be ready yet. She does not exactly want to live, since her husband despises her and the man she loves does not love her, yet has got himself into an unbearable impasse on her account. But she is not ready to die yet. All the unrest in her, all conflict, the tumultuous desire to live, be happy and be loved that rages in even the unhappiest human being, must be hushed and stilled, and "rocked asleep within [her] breast," before she can steel herself to die, and die violently. At the thought of that moment of horror, suddenly the nervous strain is intolerable; she cries out against the noise the wind is making: ". . . doors and shutters clattering / Banging and banging. . . ." These words and those that follow deepen immensely our power to imagine what it means to Kesa to die. The suggestion of cold, wild, and sad disorder without and within; the idea of death coming with the loneliest of sounds, that of wind "sighing" in the pine trees; the image of the little boat all alone far out at sea in the dark, of the rain-squall "hissing" toward her, of the sea tempestuously "heaving," yet "silent" (no help within hail) all create the idea of Kesa's state of mind: her sense of the grief, the solitude, the strangeness, the terror, the vastness of dying—of launching out alone like a boat into unfathomable mystery and blank darkness. She cannot bear the thought and cries out once again in hysterical agitation about the noises of the wind (made real by sound and rhythm), and her hysteria is augmented (illogically enough) by the thought that she might not die after all. Her husband might wake, Morito be caught, and her plan be destroyed. Presently she says to the supposed ghost:

> Do you know what I must do tonight?
> (*The Abbot is silent.*)
> Do you? (*The Abbot does not answer.*)
> I see . . . I see . . .
> How sad your silence makes me.
> Like the thought of winter coming
> And the white, cold snow in the garden
> Lying so deep and soft
> So quiet outside,
> So sad and white and still . . .
> But what else can I do?

Perhaps until this moment she has had a faint hope that something might happen to save her. But the Abbot's silence kills that hope, for she believes that, being a ghost, he knows the future. The image of the winter coming expresses with intensity her final acceptance of death. She has grown quiet and pensive: the disappearance of turmoil and active misery is suggested in words like "white," "still," and "soft" and in the picture called up of the smooth winter landscape, all protuberances and jaggednesses softened and leveled by the depth of whiteness. But "lying so soft and so deep" suggests the great depth of sorrow that spreads over everything in the world, as snow seems to do in mid-winter. The long quiet rhythm and the final question, "But what else can I do?," help to suggest her passion of sadness buried deep in the quiet of acceptance.

The poetic quality of the scene is intensified rather than diminished by such homely touches as Kesa's account of her sleeping husband, whom, because he was uncharacteristically very drunk, she was able to induce to go to bed in another room. She says Wataru is fast asleep and snoring: "So peacefully whistling like a kettle—can you hear?" This rather comic image has a strong effect. The scene before, between Kurodo and Kawachi, has presented Wataru as a man of exquisite taste and elegant manners. Here we see him as his wife sees him—exposed in an undignified but familiar aspect, rather ridiculous, and extremely real and human. This makes us understand in a flash how real he is to her and therefore how utterly impossible it would be to Kesa, however little she loves or has cause to love him, to let him be murdered. Also it suggests how safe he is, compared with Kesa; and she in her humanity has made him safe.

But let us turn to Kesa's explanation of her motive. It is, she says, that Morito may be free. She knows now that he has proposed the murder of Wataru out of pity for her; and, using a profoundly female image, she says:

> He pities me. Can love be so full of sick-pity
> That he would kill for me?
> Yet I don't scorn pity.
> To me it's like love—still-born . . .
> The shape, the size, the tenderness and frailty of what could be
> All there—exactly—
> But not alive—pitifully lolling and limp—
> As a dead child's limbs must feel in its mother's arms—
> And so nearly living—finger-nails and eyelashes formed—
> And only air—just air in-breathed—
> The first breath—
> The mindless daring of it—
> Dividing the poor wee thing from death.

The Abbot (who *is* Morito) remorsefully protests that it is Kesa who pities Morito. *Her* love is not stillborn; she can feel. It is Morito in whom there is this deadness. At this Kesa cries out in distress. Her object is, by her death, to free Morito from the entanglement with her and from the guilt feelings that have strangled his ability to live. She wants him to be free again, "To stride the hills of his mind and be merry."

The play makes Kesa's charity, which "desireth nothing," completely human and comprehensible. The scene ends with Kesa's expressing the faltering hope that some day it may comfort Morito to realize how entirely she loved him, and she hopes to be able to suffer the death stroke thinking of nothing but him. The Abbot, though he cannot stop what is past, does at last feel satisfied that Kesa's death was not utterly meaningless. As he witnesses Morito's rush into the room and what follows, he is forced to live through the killing once again, and the scene ends.

The *play* ends with the most amusing of the three Kurodo and Kawachi scenes. These two old friends are now very old men, and with their usual humor and zest for life, they agree that they find this fact of their age, themselves, and each other ridiculous. They are a little cross with Morito for insisting on their coming out on this cold autumn morning to meet him in what was Wataru's garden, as he has on this day every year for the last fifty years. Presently they realize that he is very late. Then they find him lying under the magnolia tree, dead; he is drenched with dew as if he has lain there all night. It is clear that Morito has died in the almost superhuman attempt to understand fully the murder committed fifty years before. Of course neither Kurodo nor Kawachi nor anybody else knows anything whatever about this ancient crime. The scene has grown serious. The two lightweights mourn sincerely for their dead friend, who had become a priest, and then, by rapid steps, an Abbot. They decide that his great and unique value consisted in his taking life really seriously; he was the only person who had ever taken *them* quite seriously; and for a moment they see that they themselves have been a little cowardly in never asserting their own virtues sufficiently. But the play ends with their deciding that ". . . while we're warm we must be foolish. . . ." Kurodo: "And weep sometimes when we remember / Morito, our friend / Who was also foolish once and warm. . . ." Until in the end they forget him entirely. And so the play ends.

II *Structural Principles of the Play*

This last scene has a Shakespearean function in the complex structure of the whole work, for it sets the strange, wild, unusual, sad story back in the setting of ordinary life and leaves us calm enough for the story to sink into the mind and germinate thought there. Manson's plays are built like poems. The structure is never obtrusive in the whole poetic unity of which it forms a basic part, but is often emphasized only, as in *The Noose-Knot Ballad,* by some special feature of poetic form—there, by the three ballads. When the structure of a play is so integral a part of its poetic unity, one is not always aware of the way it works. But in *The Counsellors, The Festival,* and *The Magnolia Tree* the structure is more noticeably complex and in itself forms an almost extra fascination. In *The Magnolia Tree* the first of the Abbot's two soliloquies might be shorter, but both are essential.

The structural device of the four Moritos makes the story come alive with a most vivid immediacy. The structurally cunning way the fact that it is Kesa who is killed and not Wataru is kept a secret till the last act causes an amazing denouement: the only Morito who knows the truth is the Abbot, and as we look back we see that his attitude to Kesa has been affected throughout the play by the knowledge of her sacrifice.

Then the three Kurodo and Kawachi scenes are cunningly placed. Their chief function is to throw an outside light on Morito, and at the same time, by the cleverness and charm of the two friends, their goodhearted high spirits, bubbling over with impudence, wit and humor, to lighten the tension of the play. They first appear in the middle of the first act, where their laughing eloquence about their own carefree, but "not ugly," love affairs, and their gay teasing of Morito, throw into strong relief Morito's own very different feelings. Their next appearance, late at night in the pleasure house, in the middle of the second act, is in fact, the turning point of the play, for it is they who, by their play-acting at sorrow for Wataru, cause Morito to go back to Kesa and confirm his vow of murder.

In this scene, too, the delightful happy gaiety of the antiphony they make together acts with terrific force as a contrast to the utterly different mood, character, emotional capacity, and moral stature of Morito. They take him to be merely heavily and morosely drunk. They have not the slightest inkling that he is on the verge of a dreadful decision; nor do they ever know that it is their play-acting that has pushed him over the verge. There is a tremendous weight in the irony of this fateful scene. Finally, in the last scene of all, Kurodo and Kawachi sum up Morito's character as they see it, so that, even though they know nothing of the greatest crises in his life, we are left with a more complete understanding of his value.

CHAPTER 10

Pat Mulholland's Day

"SHALL I tell you what you have that other men don't have, and that will make the future?" says Connie to Mellors in Lawrence's novel, *Lady Chatterley's Lover.* "It's the courage of your own tenderness, that's what it is." Manson, unlike most contemporary writers, has the courage "that will make the future"—if it is to be a future with any humanity in it. This tenderness that Lawrence speaks of is poles apart from sentimentality. For sentimentality, in the strictest sense, always has something false in it: it is not pure feeling, but whipped-up emotion. Tenderness, on the other hand, is something completely pure and natural that moves mysteriously within us, like a spring pushing up, almost irresistibly. Unfortunately, people do resist it, out of vanity: they are afraid of being thought "soft"—a fatal cowardice when it affects a whole civilization. For, says Henry James, feelings never expressed gradually cease to be felt. Only those who have an ingrained habit of never lying about their deepest feelings will take the risk of being laughed at for them.

I *Prologue: Intimation of the Theme*

In the Prologue to *Pat Mulholland's Day* the language is full of a kind of tenderness—the beauty of all creation, terrible and mysterious as it also is, is felt in the lines with an extraordinary delicacy of—shall we call it affection? It is clear that the poet "enjoys the world" in minute detail, in Traherne's sense of "enjoy," and in the "tenderness" with which he writes of it, there is, as in all real tenderness, an extraordinarily lively, and at the same time extraordinarily delicate, response. This same quality is constantly present also (though it by no means excludes violent anger and rigorous criticism) in the human relationships of the play proper.

Pat Mulholland's Day was published by Nasionale Boekhandel in 1964 and was produced the same year, with some éclat, by the

Iscor Dramatic Society near Pretoria. Unlike all Manson's other plays, this one is set in the present and in South Africa. "I have not included," says Manson, "any race problems. Days frequently pass in South Africa in which these temporary problems do not make themselves felt. Mulholland's problems are greater than any political ones." The play is mainly about the different kinds of courage that are needed by men, women, and children, if life is to have sense and dignity. The uneasy foreboding the Prologue produces —that Pat Mulholland's Day may possibly be his last—arouses a sharp and almost painful anxiety on his behalf before we have even seen him.

II *Opening Scenes*

Pat Mulholland, a South African of Irish descent, has won a Victoria Cross in the 1939–45 war; he is a sculptor, who, though absolutely dedicated to his art, is as yet "unsuccessful": he is just beginning to be appreciated and to scrape a living for himself, his wife May, his adolescent daughter Jenny, and his eleven- or twelve-year-old son Bogy. His Day opens early in the morning in his sculptor's studio with Mulholland cleaning his shoes, when Jenny comes in with his morning tea. From the entirely natural talk that ensues between them, partly joking, partly disagreeing, sometimes very serious, we learn a great deal (Mulholland, incidentally, does not talk down to his rather "cheeky" daughter, and he insists on her not running away from the truths that embarrass or frighten her but on her doing her best to face and express them, not to him as her "daddy," but to him as a man).

There are at least four different levels of interest in the story, all cunningly and unobtrusively mingled. There is the level of "fact": on that level, we learn that Mulholland was badly wounded in the last war—a piece of shrapnel went right through him, so close to the heart that it only just missed the aorta; that Bogy has gone, for some reason, very early to school; that Jenny too is at school and that her father is going to give her, heavy as she is now growing, a lift on his bicycle; that there is a good deal of tension in the household; that they are far from rich; and that Mulholland is going in to town to pay bills, change library books, and see about his life insurance. At the same time, on another level of interest, we came to know (surprisingly, almost uncannily well, for so much is suggested in a few touches) the personalities of the four

people in the family and their interaction upon each other. Jenny
and her mother are not particularly gifted, whereas Mulholland
and the little boy are strikingly so. This is one of the causes of
tension in the household. The two males are a little like storks in a
barnyard; the two females, despite a profound affection for them,
do not quite understand their strange natures, and because they
are a bit intimidated by Mulholland; they feel hostile and feel
themselves, sometimes defiantly, but wrongly on the whole, to be
"ordinary." Jenny understands a good deal about her little
brother, however. Mulholland understands both his womenfolk
very well, but there is at present a slight estrangement between
him and his wife, which Jenny senses, and tries clumsily to put
right. "You don't love her any more, do you?" she blurts out. Mulholland tells her that his wife loves him but that he cannot feel it
because she does not show it. She does not want him to come to
her at present, though she does not even know this. All she can do
is "Wait. She can only wait. Everything will come right." The
scene ends with a typical frustration between May and Mulholland, the ordinariness of daily life, May's reserve, and Mulholland's temper combining to prevent understanding: as he is going
out, Mulholland turns and looks at his wife. "May?" he says tenta-
tively. May looks at him, but suddenly sees something: "Oh, Pat—
your fly's undone!"

On the third level, we learn what it is that makes Mulholland a
sculptor. On the fourth, we become conscious of two images that
run through the whole play, transforming it from a merely domestic and human drama into a poem of almost transcendental significance; first, the moon image; second, the image of the estuary.

The business of being an artist of course vitally concerns both
Mulholland and the whole uncaring world. Part of Jenny is distressed because her father is so unlike other "daddies," and she
obviously wonders (as Mulholland puts it) whether "All the re-
moteness and tenseness and temper is really necessary / That a
chunk of old stone / Should be battered and chipped to tell of
flesh and bone." He tries to explain it to her, "Where d'you think
I dig these shapes from, Jenny?"

Jenny.   From the bare stone, Daddy, just like you said.

Mulholland. No. No. No. I dig them up out of darkness,
               From the terrors and dreads and darkness inside me

> And all the honey-sweet, secret joys I dare not share
> Until they've found some form.

Naturally enough, Jenny does not understand, and he tries to explain to her the humiliation of his frequent failures. But she would exult for him sometimes, he says, when he has felt himself "riding / The high-striding horse of [his] own force / Through looming dreads. . . ." For the most difficult, the most private, the most solitary, and perhaps the profoundest kind of courage man is capable of is needed for discovering some of the secrets of life, and, in doing so, giving them a form that makes them communicable to others. This most difficult kind of courage is perhaps the very kind that is most desperately needed by the human race, "because also man writhes and cannot move / Inside some kind of granite stone," the dross of which must be hacked and chipped away, so that he can be free. "That's my trade, Jenny," he says proudly.

III *Imagery*

The moon image is first used by Mulholland in trying to explain to his worried young daughter how he values his wife May. May does not care about his sculpture in itself; and she is too reserved to express her love for him. The moon "throws cool shadows" over his sculpture.

> . . . she shows me things by casting shadows
> In a way the bright sun never can.
> And so, secretly, so no one hears her, she reproves me,
> Shows me where I have been clumsy or dull . . .
> You'll laugh at me if I say your mother is like the moon to me
> And not the sun.

This image has a strange poetic power. The words suggest very strongly how deep and quiet, how veiled almost from himself as well as from her, is Mulholland's feeling for his wife. Hers for him is a love subdued like the moon's light. It suggests also those qualities in May that we get to know well in the course of the play—a certain reserved plainness and straightness; almost ordinariness, but certainly not ordinariness; a tremendous depth of latent truth, for all her inarticulateness; and a kind of natural dignity of character, though she can be clumsy and is usually diffident. (The moon image is used again about May in the last scene of the play.) May is a character whom Manson always handles most movingly. It is noteworthy that what Mulholland, who feels the meaning of life mainly in and through his work, particularly values in his by no means artistic wife is the silent way her mere presence and being show him, perhaps because of the quiet, strong truth latent in her, where he has gone wrong in his work— ". . . secretly, so no one hears her"—for she is a most loyal wife—"she reproves me / Shows me where I have been clumsy or dull."

As mysterious and pervasive in its effect is the estuary image. This first appears in the painting which Bogy has made for his father. It is a most vivid painting of "the sea—an estuary really" —of bright sand, green breakers, then "a heaving dark blue dangerous sea" beyond. Shortly before this Jenny has been talking about what they will buy if her father ever gets rich, and when she hears that the picture is of an estuary, she cries impulsively, "When we're rich we'll buy Bogy a boat." "No. No," says Mulholland, "Bogy must make his own boat / And sail it down his own river to the sea. / Poor little Bogy." There is a mingling of such deep compassion and respect, such fellow feeling for a fellow artist, such fatherly and human responsibility in this remark, that— combined with the description of the dangerous sea beyond the bright shore in Bogy's painting—it makes us feel that the estuary represents something like, perhaps, the mystery and danger of the future, ending in inevitable death, which opens out from the brightness of life into a terrible, beautiful, infinite unknown. And this image too recurs significantly again and again, especially toward the end of the Day.

IV *The Consulting Room*

From the next two scenes in Dr. Wright's consulting room, whither Mulholland has confidently gone to get the medical certificate required for renewing his life insurance, we learn that he is a doomed man. The hole made by the piece of shrapnel has made the wall of the aorta wear as thin as tissue paper, and any violent exertion on Mulholland's part may break it at any time. Mulholland has been feeling exceptionally well and healthy. Moreover, he confesses to the doctor that he feels growing within him, like an absolute certainty, a glorious conviction that he is on the point of producing the loveliest and most wonderful piece of work that he has ever done. The irony of this is almost too much for the sensitive Dr. Wright, a man capable of passion and generosity. He feels the dreadfulness of the news he has had to give Mulholland with a special keenness, for his wife and Mulholland were lovers before their respective marriages, and he knows that his wife still loves Mulholland. In his feelings towards his patient there is therefore a mingling of jealous pain, strong compassion, and genuine liking. For it is the essence of Mulholland's personality that because of his insight, directness, and honesty, he has a way of appealing to the best in everyone. This is shown again and again in the play.

Dr. Wright has learned through his wife to think of Mulholland as a man eminently "capable of sheer merry glee," who can also be "Suddenly terrible / —As full of grief as God himself sometimes." He is famous in the town not as an artist ("they wouldn't care if he was Leonardo himself") but as its only Victoria Cross medal owner. But now he is afraid, and in what Mulholland says, Manson makes us feel vividly the wildness of his terror. No one finds it easy to be brave. Courage, says Mulholland, every kind of courage, for there is really only one kind, is a matter of "you do or you don't"; and how can you know beforehand whether you will or you won't? Wright suggests that he should tell his wife, but he cannot: for the time being all they have endured together "Has shrunk into something withered and small"; if there were time they would endure this winter as plants do, and a green time might come again. But *now*, how can he tell her that the green time will never come again? Dr. Wright is sure that Mulholland will still manage to express in sculpture the glorious thing that he feels to be within him. Presently, Mulholland's courage returns and he says, "I'll live as calm and as long as I can / As cool as a stone / That lichen and soft moss grow on." Alas, this calm is to be utterly denied him.

V   *At Mulholland's Studio*

Arriving at his studio in midafternoon, Mulholland finds Jenny there in a difficult and defiant mood, saying stupid, insolent things to her father about his statuary and about "culture" in general. We see Mulholland talking to her quite seriously as a fellow human

being, for he is a man whose understanding of people includes
children and adolescents. Throughout the play we are given remarkably convincing pictures of his excellent, though at times ab-
sent-minded, way of dealing with them. Quite unsentimental,
radically patient despite his surface impatience and flashes of violent temper, he decidedly has "the courage of his tenderness," so
that although May and Jenny are afraid of him—because of something dark and deep in him that comes from his overriding passion for those profound life values that one might call eternal—yet
people can speak to him more honestly and fully than to anybody
else. Between Mulholland and May, however, this kind of confidence is at present suspended, and May is extremely, though silently, unhappy because of this. Manson's domestic dialogue is
completely natural; yet it is never "small beer," for the people
engaged in it are not petty people, and their central interests are
profound and real.

Jenny, despite her special understanding of her much younger
brother, is jealous of Mulholland's interest in him, and he talks to
her honestly and affectionately. He does not love Bogy more than
he loves her, but he worries more about him—because "he is
really an artist." To be an artist, explains Mulholland, "You've just
got to be . . . very brave, that's all," and he explains that it takes
courage to look at things properly; really seeing things is "so
frightening at first," for one sees that terror is an essential part of
beauty and helps to make it.

At this point Mrs. Mulholland returns from the "hen party" she
has been to, and Jenny rushes out of the room to hide her recent
tears, colliding with her in the doorway. May is slightly drunk and
is defiant about it. She assumes that Mulholland has been "getting
at" Jenny: he will not allow either her or Jenny to be "ordinary,"
as they were meant to be. "For God's sake let her be," she shouts.
"What are you trying to make her, eh? / (blazing with anger)
What the hell did you try to make me?" Then she softens and asks
whether he has paid the bills he went out to pay. "And did you fix
up about the insurance?" "Yes, that's finished with. Over and
done," he replies, with an irony of which May, of course, has no
inkling. "Oh well, that's something anyway," she says; "At least
we won't starve if you die." Immediately she repents of her unfeeling words, but of course they hurt him far more than she can

guess. Unhappy, slightly tipsy, and now stung with guilt, she bursts out:

> Oh God, what's the use? What's the use, eh, Patrick?
> How many years are you going on with this?
> You're getting *old*, Pat! Can't you see, can't you see?
> Maybe someone should tell you . . .

Mulholland. (*icily*). . . . What? . . .

May. (*crying and shouting angrily at the same time*).
That you're no bloody good! That's all, that's all . . .
No bloody good at all!
(*There is an absolute silence. She looks at him with horror.*)
Oh Christ! Pat! I'm sorry. I'm sorry . . .
Oh Pat, I'm sorry.

Mulholland. That's O.K., May . . .

May. I'm terribly sorry . . .

Mulholland. That's O.K., May.

May. (*heartbroken*). It's not true!

Mulholland. That's O.K., May.

There is a depth of dumb and mutual grief in this exchange: in May's commonplace words, unexpressed and inexpressible shame and penitence; in Mulholland's, silent, unapproachable hurt. The scene ends with Mulholland turning away and changing into his working coat, while May looks on, longing but not daring and not knowing how to comfort him.

The next scene shows May and Jenny preparing supper and taking special pains to please Mulholland, for each feels guilty toward him. May is harrowed with penitence, and Jenny, for all her impudence, is very fond of her father. While working, Jenny talks to her mother about her father and Bogy, and the image of the estuary, which is a secret bond between Mulholland and the little boy, comes in again. Bogy has often talked to Jenny about this estuary so that she vividly imagines it. The idea of it is "sort of secret and terrible and strange":

> . . . bright—sort of leaping bright and spiteful
> Like water in a stream . . .
> Going on and on falling downwards and frothing,
> Churning and chuckling with a sort of frenzy—on and on
> Until it begins to go slow and run muddy,
> Winding and widening—out and out
> Like an estuary running into the sea . . .
> And there's nothing but marshes and mudbanks and reeds
> And sea-birds calling, light and clear,
> And far away the sea . . .
> And somehow that makes them terribly unhappy.

Bogy and Mulholland share the knowledge of this estuary and can both imitate the sound of the birds there exactly. May is disturbed. Her comment, "Poor little Bogy," echoes Mulholland's when he speaks of Bogy as an artist. May desperately wants to know more, but Jenny can only tell her that sometimes Mulholland, when excited about this vision, makes little boats of expensive, thick red paper, and shouts to Bogy, "I'm making them! I'm making them!," upon which man and boy stick the boats in their pockets and go off, if no one is watching, to the river. The image is full of brilliant sensuous life, through which a remarkably strong though indefinable sense of its import is conveyed: in it is an acute apprehension of life *sub specie aeternitatis*, as in the Prologue, and of the intense sadness of being vividly aware at one and the same moment of the joy of life and of its ending in death. Yet in the realization of this bitter fact there is felt to be a kind of mysterious and religious beauty, a submission to something immeasurably greater than ourselves and infinitely beyond us. The mysterious and complex intimations of the image are so fused in the poetry that analysis can hardly separate and name them.

Muholland and Bogy are both late for supper; and the best efforts of the two womenfolk to make it a pleasant occasion are foiled, for when Mulholland—still deeply wounded, and, of course, violently disturbed in secret by the doctor's news—sits down, Jenny, in tossing a salad, spills the oil on his trousers. His temper blazes up, and in the ensuing fuss he utters a few home

truths in a mood of extremely bitter and jeering irony. Jenny has
been insolent, and Pat has flicked the dishtowel in her face so that
it's really stung. May has tried to intervene: "You'll hurt her."
"Hurt *her?*," cries Mulholland "I'll only hurt myself, May," and
remembering his mortal danger, he sits down; when he speaks
again it is very quietly: "Come then, let's sit down, shall
we? / Like one big, happy family / That's what I like about fami-
lies, Jenny, don't you, May? / They never really mean what they
say, do they?" He speaks with corroding irony about how he
"really should be a bank clerk and earn safe money." Being a
sculptor "is rather selfish, isn't it, May?"

> (*With bitter sarcasm*) Oh, not *really*, of course . . .
> (*angrily*) Nor is it noble or brave or true
> To do what you think you have to do! . . .
> Silly old Daddy for *using* such words!
> They're all jokes *really*, Jenny!
> And it's really only a *joke* in a way for poor old Daddy to
>   say . . .
> He's sick and tired of it all—of you too, Jenny,
> And Mummy as well,
> Because, you see, she frankly bores him sometimes . . .
> Oh not *really*, Jenny,
> It's just a funny sort of family joke!

Then suddenly he is quiet; all the "anger and spite and vengeful-
ness" go out of him, and with an authority that neither Jenny nor
May dare resist, he commands silence to everybody and goes off
to work "in silence" while they clear and wash up "in silence."
"Something terrible's happened to him to-day," says May. "I
know. I just know. Sooner or later he'll tell me about it." Suddenly
through the window Jenny notices Bogy lying under a tree, crying,
and in spite of Jenny's telling her that he will hate her for it, May
rushes out to see what is wrong.

   As the curtain goes up again Mulholland is working, unnatu-
rally absorbed and intent, in his studio, and a short and moving
scene follows that shows how hurt Mulholland is, how contrite
May. He cannot look at May, Pat explains, for if he did he would
see quite plainly "That you love me / And that would make me
feel very, very sorry for myself." "And I must work now, May," he

says. Presently he turns around. "There! That's over!!" he says. "What is it, May?" and May replies she wants to talk to him about Bogy.

There follows a masterly passage, extremely comical though highly charged with painful emotion. May is so upset about Bogy and so much afraid that Patrick will influence him in a direction she fears that it takes some time for the story to emerge through the thick tangle of illogicalities and absurd contradictions in which her emotions involve it. Bogy is being bullied by a great strong brute of a boy called Thompson, and May is terrified that Mulholland will expect her son, a "tiny little thin boy," to fight him. "He's been bullied and beaten," cries May, almost hysterically. "Beaten!" shouts Mulholland, leaping off the bed. (He is lying down because May has asked him to sit down, saying "You're always more reasonable sitting down, somehow," and amused and good-tempered, he has lain down instead.) When Mulholland shouts "Beaten!" in indignation, May has perforce to withdraw: "Not exactly beaten—because he's had the sense to run away." Mulholland, full of sympathy for his little son, knows he has been running away for a long time, but he has not, as May suspects, advised him to fight. But "I did say this May: I said it quite seriously / I said, If you run away you won't get hurt / And if you fight, you will. . . ." And, says Pat, "I think he saw my point."

Mulholland is agonized at the thought that poor Bogy *will* run away, and when May in a passionate rage, misunderstands him and thinks he only cares about the *disgrace* of it, he too is passionately angry, for what he is afraid of is what running away will do to Bogy. He knows exactly how frightened Bogy is, he says, and his words show that he does. A furious and interesting argument follows, which shows that May at the moment and against her better knowledge cares only about Bogy's getting hurt, but Mulholland understands the issues involved with a much greater objectivity and depth of insight. "Let him be cowardly!" cries May, in a passion. "Yes, if he wants to be," says Mulholland. "How can he *want* to be?" cries May, too angry to see where the argument is taking her. "Who ever *wants* to be?" Presently, when Mulholland asks her whether she wants Bogy to be cowardly, she is trapped into saying, "Let him be what he *wants* to be." "That's all I want, May," says Mulholland. "I'll ask him what he wants to be." "If you do," cries May, in a fury, "I'll hate and despise you forever!!" She is so enraged at her total failure to find arguments in favor of cowardice that, quite beside herself, she shouts abuse at him. "Do you know what *you* are?" Mulholland shouts back, and when she defies him to tell her, suddenly he laughs, "tenderly and surprisingly." "A female!" he says. May stops in her tracks; then she gives him a resounding slap on the cheek and runs out of the room.

She is hardly gone when Jenny comes in, "bouncing and flouncing," as Mulholland puts it, "And flashing and gnashing teeth at me." She too is intent on "saving" Bogy from Mulholland, but when Bogy comes in, she turns on him for "sucking round Daddy," jeering cruelly at him in an attempt to convince him that he will not be able to face the bully. Mulholland turns her out of the room and talks to Bogy with the profoundest sympathy and understanding, leaving him perfectly free in his mind to avoid the fight to which, it appears, he has desperately challenged Thompson. But he speaks in such a way that Bogy realizes the truth of a favorite saying of Mulholland's, "It's either you fight or you die— you do what you must do, / Or you don't—and die." Though Mulholland says "never promise," Bogy promises to fight Thompson, and in a state of feverish anxiety, he begs his father to go with him. "I want to go now, now," says Bogy afraid resolution may fade, and Mulholland fully understands. As they go out of the room, Bogy takes his father's hand.

VI *Dialogue and Characterization*

The three episodes of this scene are extremely natural, real, and moving. The dialogue, which appears absolutely spontaneous, with not an unusual word or a polysyllable in it, is so packed with the thoughts and feelings and situation of each of the four characters and with their development—as passions, sympathies, and ideas clash together—that it has been extremely difficult to give any kind of adequate summary of it. As well as this, there are numerous unobtrusive, subtle touches in that small space that have made us see into each character surprisingly well, and we find ourselves warmly liking and strongly concerned for every one of them. Their speeches could not be spoken by anybody of a different age or sex from themselves. Every sentence is what only that particular character could have spoken. Bogy, for all his possible genius, is only a little boy, and a brave one, in his terror and his tears and his pride, and in the way he hits out at his sister, and puts both arms around his father, clinging to him. Jenny is a difficult teen-ager, presumptuous, impertinent, and impetuous, but with a great capacity for affection and much hidden delicacy and intuition. May is a female whose illogicality and temper and passionate love for her husband and children make us often almost weep as we laugh. And our respect for Mulholland, who has so much patience underneath his "temperament," greatly deepens.

VII   *Act Three*

The third act begins in an empty street near Bogy's school; in the near background is a pub. Mulholland and Bogy enter together, Bogy terrified almost out of his wits, Mulholland agonized for him and longing to hold him back. When Bogy is gone and Mulholland is in the pub to get cigarettes, three ducktails enter, half dancing, half skipping, fairly drunk, and under the influence of drugs. An episode of acute suspense follows. It is immediately obvious from their slangy talk, in a lingo that reflects the mindlessness, vicious irresponsibility and sadistic bullying of their type, that armed as they are with flick-knives and false courage they are highly dangerous. When "swinging high" after a few drags on their marijuana cigarettes, they suddenly find that they have no more of them, and no money either. Desperate, they decide to rob someone.

Just at this moment, Mulholland emerges from the pub with his new cigarettes. Managing to cut off his exit to right and left and into the pub they proceed to try and bully Pat into giving them first his cigarettes, then his money, then his wristwatch. Mulholland, knowing that if he fights he will instantly die, manages with enormous self-control to keep perfectly calm and submissive. "Why don't you blow, Dad?" urges the weakest of them nervously. "I'm staying here," says Mulholland calmly, for he has promised Bogy to wait for him. "How yellow do you have to be?" they jeer. "As yellow as is necessary," responds Mulholland, quite seriously, and when one of them called Les spits in his face, he calmly wipes it off. But when Les shouts "Don't wipe!" Mulholland quietly goes on wiping; "I said I was as yellow as is necessary —that's all," he remarks. The touch of "maniacal fury" in his voice makes the ducktail relize that Mulholland will suffer no further insult, so instead he demands Pat's jacket. As Mulholland obediently takes it off, Bogy appears and shouts "Daddy!" in horror. The ducktails, fearing other intervention, fly. Bogy has obviously lost the fight. "But I didn't run away," he cries, and not believing Mulholland's "Nor did I, Bogy, nor did I," he runs off bitter with disillusionment. The irony of this hits Mulholland so hard that he sits down on the pavement in despair, head in hands.

Meanwhile, the whole episode has been watched surreptitiously by a man inside the pub. This person, a little, sandy, bald man, now emerges, and sits down next to Mulholland. He is Curly Mac-Harry, and he and Pat were together, for a short time, in the war. Curly is now, as he admits, a hopeless alcoholic and tramp. He soon falls into talk about the war and common soldier friends, who "bought it," or who have survived, and presently he is telling Pat about a most harrowing experience of his own. This story in its tragic irony is very like what has just happened to Pat, for Curly too was once judged to be a coward, because of the failure of an attack he had led, when he was no such thing. Curly had, we discover, been very brave, but his men had been killed, wounded, or sick, and *he* had been so sick with jaundice as to be hardly conscious, so he was very slow. But so high are a soldier's standards of courage that he has never felt sure whether he was not really "yellow," and the sickness only an excuse. "You did all right, Curly," says Pat, and Curly is comforted.

This story comes out naturally and dramatically in an exchange of remarks and questions, slow at first, then warming into coherence. It is entirely men's talk; they are sharing the bottle Curly has brought with him out of the pub. Their language is soldier's language, full of the profanities and understatement of those from whom an almost impossible degree of courage is expected.

In the intimacy born of these wartime memories, Pat tells Curly what a dreadfully precarious hold he has on life, and Curly understands the whole episode of the ducktails. Presently Curly tells Pat that he's "buggered too"—with cirrhosis of the liver—the "last stage." "I'm bloody scared, Pat," he confesses. "I'm alone, you see.' They say it's a bloody awful, / Disgusting, disgraceful way to die." We feel the innate pride of Curly in that terrifying word "disgraceful."

And when Curly discovers that Pat has not told his wife about his danger, he strongly advises him to do so at once. He did not tell *his* wife from pride lest she would think his story was "all drunk talk and excuses" for being an "alky," which he was (but not, as she thought, because of the war). She would have put up with him, as women will, because she would think he was no good and protest would be of no use. "I wasn't, you see," he asserts, with his proud sense of honor. "So I just drunk myself half dead instead." Now his wife has left him and he has lost touch with his children; he is alone. He begs Pat not to make the same mistake: "Tell her you're dead, man, finished and through / That the slightest thing will kill you / Let her look at you and see—"

> *Mulholland.* What will she see?
>
> *Curly.*   (*spiritedly*). What anyone can see—
>   You can do what you have to do—
>   And you're brave—like me.
>   As brave as any man can be!

Moved by affectionate insight into Curly's indomitable character and by a strong feeling of comradeship, Mulholland persuades this isolated derelict to go home with him. It is like Mulholland to do this, and like Curly to accept. Mulholland helps Curly to his feet, and they go off together.

An hour or so later we see Pat and Curly entering Mulholland's studio slightly drunk. Mulholland is going to tell his family the truth, and then, he says "—we'll have a party." "Can't you see they'll all be terribly upset?" protests Curly.

> *Mulholland.* (*helping himself to another drink*). Of course they
>   will be,
>   But life beats on. It beats on and on until it's done!
>   And I'm the heart of this house, Curly,
>   So we'll beat the drum and we'll dance and sing,
>   Because life beats on and we all belong . . .

"To what?" asks Curly. "To mankind's lousy, raggle-taggle army! / We still belong! We all belong!

This simple colloquial exchange, with its careless, rough rhythm, suggesting the bravado and spirit and the inextinguishable gaiety of Mulholland and Curly, expresses the same inexhaustible power and wonder of life which are celebrated in the

Prologue, and which underlie all Mulholland says of why he is a sculptor. Mulholland, at home in his own house, is the heart of his house, and he feels that power and wonder in his own physical heart, especially now that it is mortally threatened. After making Curly comfortable with drink and an easy chair, Mulholland goes off to tell his family the bad news about himself. "We'll teach them," says Mulholland to Curly, "what we used to be, and what we still are / 'Cos it's true. We still are something! / At least we can still die gay, eh, Curly?" To which Curly replies affectionately, "You crazy, drunk bastard!"—soldiers' language that manages, somehow, to be entirely adequate to the situation.

The very strong feeling these two ex-soldiers have acquired for each other is based partly on the similarity of their situations, for they are walking right into the darkness of death, together, as it were; partly on the natural pride and dignity they both have; and partly on their both having been mistaken for cowards when they were being brave. This profound sense of comradeship between these two very unconventional people is expressed with unobtrusive subtlety in every part of their ordinary-sounding language.

VIII *Final Scene*

Three or four hours later the party is over, Bogy has long been asleep in bed, and Curly is sound asleep in an armchair in the studio. Mulholland is quite drunk, May slightly so, and even Jenny is a little tipsy. There is a dreamy, profoundly meditative air about the whole scene. Mutual trust and affection among all the people in the house seem to radiate a kind of warmth and even happiness that make the extreme sadness of the situation for all of them at least not a bleak sadness. Obviously the tale has been told, and May and Jenny have taken it heroically and joined in the party with the genuine gaiety of those who can be stoical when occasion calls. Now, with the lively agreement of people who have for many years shared and delighted in much of their daily lives together, they talk of domestic details of the past. A hundred delicate touches unobtrusively create a beautiful tone. The estuary image and the moon image reappear. For Mulholland suddenly calls for the expensive red paper and begins to make four little boats, one for each of them— "and [one for] Curly too." Tomorrow they will sail them. They look at Curly, and Mulholland, who like all good artists is extremely observant, and has, moreover, an exceptional capacity for affectionate and imaginative interest in others, says to May:

> . . . Look at his shiny, bald head . . .
> What's he thinking of, dreaming of . . . ?
> Oh, May . . . May! His mother ruffled his hair . . . it was soft
> . . . and curly . . .
> It was curly . . . Where's Curly? Where is he?
> (to Jenny) Look carefully, can you see? Can you see . . . ?
> He has a fine head, can you see?
> Most people's heads don't sit so nicely, so firmly—
> So square and true—
> As if you felt his backbone run up straight—right through
> him . . .

He draws attention to how "Sort of neat and tight and tough—and stubborn—can you see?" from pride, Curly is "In that funny sort of way gay men / With a sort of speed of life in them can be."

In every touch this speech is a sculptor's—not a painter's—a sculptor's, with his practiced eye and hand that deal in three dimensions. It is also the speech of a most human human being, possessing a great depth of altruistic emotion; it is the speech of a brave man who has worked hard for courage and loves it in others. We see that it is partly Mulholland's courage and affection that have enabled May and Jenny to bear what they have to bear. The simplicity of the scene is warm with the living life inside it. But it is bedtime, and Mulholland gets up, staggering a little. He asks May to fetch water and a bottle of whiskey to put beside Curly in his veranda bed, for he will need both when he wakes.

Then, while she is out of the room, suddenly a terrifying thing happens. Mulholland wakes Curly—"bedtime, bedtime, bedtime, boy!"—and as Curly tries to walk to the veranda he staggers, Mulholland instinctively catches him, picks him up, and begins to carry him out to his bed on the veranda. "Daddy, Daddy, put him down, put him down!" shouts Jenny, terrified, but Mulholland goes on carrying the now unconscious man out to his bed. Jenny's panic-stricken shouts bring her mother running. May comes in in dread, fearing the worst, but the next moment, Mulholland walks back into the room, unconcerned. "You fool! You mad fool!" cries

TWAYNE'S WORLD AUTHORS SERIES

A Survey of the World's Literature

Sylvia E. Bowman, Indiana University

GENERAL EDITOR

SOUTH AFRICA

Joseph Jones, University of Texas

EDITOR

H. W. D. Manson

(*TWAS 220*)

H. W. D. Manson

By CHRISTINA VAN HEYNINGEN and C. O. GARDNER

University of Natal

Twayne Publishers, Inc.   ::   New York

Preface

Of this book, two parts, the chapters on *The Festival* and on *Potluck*, have been written by Mr. C. O. Gardner, and the rest by me. This disproportion is mainly due to the fact that, having retired, I had the leisure, and Mr. Gardner had not. But Mr. Gardner has collaborated also in my share by listening to me read each chapter as I finished it and by making valuable criticisms and suggestions. He has also drawn up the chronology and the bibliography and has been kind enough to undertake most of the drudgery inevitable in preparing a manuscript for the press. For various facts about our author's life I am indebted to his mother, Mrs. D. Manson, and his elder brother, Mr. Leonard Manson, M.C.

A South African writing for the theater today must look forward to starvation unless he can contrive to alternate periods of earning a living in some other way with long spells of continuous and intense concentration on his writing. This Manson, being determined and tenacious, and no "hands-upper," managed to do. Professional theater hardly exists in South Africa except for the four provincial government-aided companies, for Cape, Free State, Natal, and Transvaal, and both it and the amateur theaters are interested mainly in box-office success. There is no Bantu theater at all. English-language drama has far less chance of success than Afrikaans. In Afrikaans the indigenous theater, apart from the excellent original plays by Uys Krige, his translations of Shakespeare, some translations by other people of Molière (highly popular and well done), Chekhov and Anouilh, and one or two fine poetic plays by N. P. van Wyk Louw, concerns itself largely, even at this date, with the Boer War. Serious English-speaking playwrights, on the other hand, are expected to write about nothing but the color question, and there has been nothing of real value on that subject, except perhaps the American musicals based on two of Alan Paton's novels, but these have not come to South Africa. His delightful short story, "Sponono," has also been successfully dramatized in this mode. A play or two of Guy Butler's has had glimpses of poetry and reality but no sustained depth; and Atholl Fugard has been much boosted, but in our opinion his work, about society's colored outcasts, is contemptibly feeble, false, dull, and undramatic. The interest of the color question is too soon exhausted, too unavoidably political, too narrow, and too fashionable a theme to have employed all of Manson's considerable energies of mind, though few men of our age had more capacity for understanding people of a different race from his own. Ambitious intellectuals among South African dramatists, whether English, like Atholl Fugard, or Afrikaans, have been trying to imitate the British theater of the absurd, and box-office comedies (amateur or professional) are usually imitations of London West End successes.

South African plays are hardly looked at overseas unless they exploit the fashionable color question. (How many people who ride that hobbyhorse are a thousandth part as much interested in its realities as Manson was?) Besides this, there is still a good deal of very deep unconscious English snobbery there (as well as in English-speaking Southern Africa) about "colonials." Your true-born Englishman simply cannot believe in his heart of hearts that any "colonial" can possibly be as good as an Englishman, let alone better! Nevertheless, as we relate elsewhere, Manson's work has been greatly admired by a few of the most eminent British actors and scholars of our time, two of his plays were produced in Britain, others had been accepted in Britain, America, and Canada, where one had been broadcast and options bought on others. All the plays, by the way, have been staged or broadcast, or both, in South Africa.

The critical method we employ in this book, which has been at least half consciously and often wordlessly employed by all good readers of literature from time immemorial, is that specifically initiated by Dr. F. R. Leavis, Dr. I. A. Richards, Mr. R. G. Biaggini and others, and adumbrated by Stephen Potter in his very interesting book, *The Muse in Chains*—that is, the method of "Practical Criticism." Assuming (what surely ought to be axiomatic) that the important thing about a work of literature is the book itself—not the author's life and ideas, not what people think of his work, what trends it reflects, and all the rest of it, but the book itself and the impact it makes in its living wholeness upon a qualified reader—we have devoted nearly all our attention to giving those people who have read Manson not at all, or only partially, or have forgotten what they have read, a *living* idea of each play we discuss. In other words, we have tried to make it, though at second hand, enter "alive into the heart," as Wordsworth says poetry should. With this purpose in mind, we have quoted as much as there was room for, commenting on what each quotation achieves and how it does so, and we have tried to tell the story in such a way as to approach, as nearly as possible, the effect made by the original play, and to make our summaries include as much interpretation and implied criticism as possible. In this attempt we hope we have not been altogether unsuccessful, and we hope that it will lead the uninitiated and the partly initiated to acquire and read Manson's plays for themselves and that it will inspire producers to give these plays, by means of first-rate productions, something of the fullness of life that they were created for.

C. v. H.

Acknowledgments

We have to thank the publishers for permission to quote from Manson's plays: A. A. Balkema, of Cape Town and Amsterdam, for *The Festival*; Human and Rousseau, of Cape Town, for *The Green Knight, Captain Smith,* and *The Noose-Knot Ballad*; Nasionale Boekhandel, of Parow, for *The Magnolia Tree* and *Pat Mulholland's Day*; and the University of Natal Press, of Pietermaritzburg, for *The Counsellors* and *Potluck*. For their services we wish to thank our typists, Mrs. Hill and Mrs. Patzer, and for criticism and encouragement, Mr. and Mrs. Jonathan Crewe.

We also wish to thank *Theoria* for permission to reprint *Unposted Letter* and the prologue to *Pat Mulholland's Day*.

Contents

Chronology

1926 Harley Manson born on January 29, at Tabora, Tanganyika (now Tanzania).
1931 Attends infant school at Dar-es-Salaam.
1933 Family moves to England. Manson later attends school at Chatham House, Ramsgate.
1939 Move to South Africa.
1940 Attends school at Saint Andrew's College, Grahamstown.
1944–1945 Serves with the Royal Natal Carbineers in Italy.
1946 Becomes a student at the University of Witwatersrand, Johannesburg.
1950 Writes *The Fight at Finnsburgh*.
1951 Temporary lecturer at the University of Natal in Pietermaritzburg. Writes *The Green Knight*. Marries Margaret Evans.
1953 Tours Europe. Writes *The Noose-Knot Ballad*.
1954 Lecturer at the University of Stellenbosch.
1955 Writes *The Counsellors. The Green Knight* produced at the University of Natal, Pietermaritzburg.
1956 *The Noose-Knot Ballad* produced at the Cygnet Theatre, Pietermaritzburg.
1956–1957 Writes *The Festival*.
1957–1958 Writes *Captain Smith*.
1958 Lecturer at the University of South Africa, Pretoria.
1960 Writes *The Magnolia Tree*.
1962 Lecturer at the University of Natal, Pietermaritzburg. *The Noose-Knot Ballad* produced by the Canadian Broadcasting Corporation.
1963 Writes *Pat Mulholland's Day*. Awarded the Olive Schreiner

Prize. *The Magnolia Tree* produced by the South African Broadcasting Corporation.

1964   *The Counsellors* produced at the University of Natal, Pietermaritzburg. *Pat Mulholland's Day* produced by the Iscor Dramatic Society, Pretoria. Awarded the Hofmeyr Prize.

1965   Visits England on an Ernest Oppenheimer travel grant. Writes *Potluck*. *Pat Mulholland's Day* produced by the South African Broadcasting Corporation.

1966   *The Magnolia Tree* produced at the Royal Lyceum Theatre, Edinburgh. *Captain Smith* produced by the South African Broadcasting Corporation.

1967   *The Magnolia Tree* published in the international theater magazine, *Gambit*. Writes *Magnus*. Marries Eleanore Kriener. *Potluck* produced (by Manson himself) at the University of Natal, Pietermaritzburg.

1968   *The Festival* produced at the University of York, England. Birth of a daughter, Kirsten.

1969   Killed in a road accident on May 29. *Magnus* produced at the University of Natal, Pietermaritzburg.

1970   Manson Memorial Fund established. Simultaneous publication of *The Counsellors, The Festival, Magnus* and *Potluck*.

1971   *Karl Gunter Hoffmann* published.

CHAPTER 1

Tone of Voice

I *South Africa Today*

ALL English South Africans, like the subject of this book, belong to at least two civilizations, that of Britain and that of South Africa. The present South African government detests this fact and is using every device of propaganda to make these South Africans renounce their British loyalties. But their British heritage is invaluable to most of them; and strongly as Manson, for example, objected to much government policy—especially that which discriminates against individuals on grounds of color alone or interferes with education—he would have freely admitted that he owed much to South Africa, and was glad to live in it.

English South Africans inherit from Britain mainly the great imaginative literature of the past, huge and varied as it is, and the values our British ancestors taught us. Shakespeare belongs to us as much as to any Englishman; so do Chaucer, Milton, Wordsworth, Lawrence, and the rest; we have been reading the great eighteenth- and nineteenth-century novelists all our lives, as well as the popular novelists of Edwardian and Georgian times and later, and our ideas of greatness and of virtue are based largely on the imaginary characters they have created and on the real ones of British history and biography. When we go to London for the first time we recognize parts of it as if we had been there before, and the names of streets there are often more familar to many of us than the houses in the small South African villages where we spent our childhood. Our imaginations are thoroughly accustomed to gray days, dark winters, mist, fog, perpetual rain, and deep ice and snow.

Yet we live in a very different kind of country, huge and still comparatively empty, but not long ago much emptier and wilder. Large tracts of it are very dry, and it is nearly always full of sunshine everywhere; it is peopled, where it is peopled, by human

15

beings, black, white and coloured,* whose lives and natures differ
greatly from those of the British. Life was very rough for everybody here not long ago, and people were hardy; and everything is
not yet tamed and subdued even for the whites. The landscape
nearly everywhere—whether flat and endless, like the Karoo or
Free State, or mountainous like the Western Cape, the Basutoland
or the Drakensberg border, or the Eastern Transvaal—is vast,
wild, and beautiful. Even the green part of Natal, which in summer is greener than Ireland and almost as fertile as the tropics, is
still comparatively wild; so that when we go to England, the very
trees look civilized to us, as ours do not. The sky here is very high:
immense heights of blue air stretch endlessly above us, and clouds
are as huge as continents. Both at night, when the stars are very
bright, and by day, one can, in most parts of the country, posi-
tively see the round earth moving in space, and see how fast it
seems to roll away from the sun by day. The stars in their constel-
lations wheel past at night as a stationary train seems to rush past
a moving one. On the thoughtful mind this kind of landscape has
a profound effect—the kind of effect very subtly and beautifully
suggested by Tolstoy in *War and Peace,* when he is reporting a
long questing discussion between Pierre and Prince André about
God and a future life. They are standing on the bank of a river,
and Tolstoy concludes the passage as follows:

Prince André did not reply. The carriage and horses had long been
led out on to the further bank, and were already harnessed, the sun
was half-sunken beneath the horizon, and the evening frost was beginning to incrust the little pools on the shore with starry crystals,
while Pierre and André, to the astonishment of the servants, coachmen
and ferry-men, still stood in the boat talking.

If God and the future life exist, then truth and virtue exist; and
man's highest happiness consists in striving for their attainment. One
must live, said Pierre, one must love, one must believe that we live
not merely now on this patch of earth, but that we have lived and
shall live eternally there in the universe. He pointed to the sky.

Prince André stood leaning on the rail of the ferry-boat and listening to Pierre. He never moved his eyes, but gazed at the red reflection
of the sun in the dark-blue flood. Pierre ceased speaking. All was

* In South Africa this word means of mixed blood, with some white
blood.

silent. The ferry-boat lay drifted along the bank, and only the ripples of the current could be heard lapping feebly against its sides. Prince André fancied that this patter of the water babbled a refrain to Pierre's words, "That is sooth, accept it: that is sooth, accept it." *

The passage suggests powerfully, yet by the most delicate means, the effect of the landscape upon the two men. They are both absorbed in a deeply serious and thoughtful discussion that is quite untouched by the trivialities of everyday life. It is not the kind of subject that would be likely to crop up on a street pavement in the middle of Birmingham, for example, nor is the mood in it the kind of mood that would be likely to possess two men in such circumstances. They would probably argue and score debating points. But, " 'there in the universe' [says Pierre]. He pointed to the sky"; and Tolstoy makes us feel that these two men are indeed surrounded, not by mere land and sky, but, almost visibly, by the whole vast inexplicable universe and by whatever mysterious force or spirit it is that informs it. This presence cannot be ignored: wherever the two men cast their absent glance, it is there, and part of its being silently enters deep into their souls. It is not like an African landscape: such details, with their strange wintry sadness, as, "the evening frost was beginning to incrust the little pools on the shore with starry crystals," or, "he never moved his eyes, but gazed at the red reflection of the sun in the dark-blue flood," make us feel vividly its cold Northern and Russian quality. But, like Africa, the landscape is essentially vast and wild and empty, a landscape in which mundane concerns are apt to drop away from the thoughtful mind, and where it seems unnatural to deny the kind of knowledge that the current "lapping feebly against the sides of the ferry-boat" seems to utter.

II *Language and Emotional Coloring*

From Britain Manson has been fortunate enough to inherit the great tradition of literature: poetry, drama, history, and novel. He is, in fact, very much more a part of it than any well-known British-born playwright or novelist I know of writing in England today. But he has spent most of his life in this great, thinly populated, untamed continent of Africa. This is partly, I think, what

---

* Translation from R. Bridges' anthology *The Spirit of Man*.

has made it impossible for him to fall into the arid nihilism of
successful plays like *Waiting for Godot,* or the blinkered domestic
dullness and squalid pettiness, and the sterile insincerity of the
Kitchen Sink school. A profound awareness of the infinite life of
"unknown modes of being" in which our little world is suspended
pervades all his plays and is most explicit in the very beautiful
Prologue to *Pat Mulholland's Day:*

> Now that you are settled and still,
> The house lights doused and dim,
> Make your minds like this dim darkness
> And bring up into it the smallest speck,
> The tiniest mote or atom it can think of—tip and touch
> And yet hold some memory of so doing—
> And imagine it
> Spinning and spinning in empty space.
> Then say this spinning speck
> Is our whole world—in one perspective.
>
> Ridiculous that it should spin
> Being flung off so long ago
> From another star or other speck
> That still is spinning, I suppose, somewhere—
> Or exploded—long ago—gone—
> In a silent white blast we never heard
> Or ever shall see,
> Although that blast may be
> What will blow our world away one day.
>
> Yet this day our little world still spins . . .
> Magnify this mote or speck and what do we see?
> It is dark on the one side away from the sun,
> Silver bright, it seems, on the other,
> And spinning and spinning continuously . . .
>
> And on that mote or speck are men—millions of them—
> Infinitesimal animals—
> Who crawl upon its surface and cling
> To life and this atom as it spins
> Through day and night
> Dark and light
> And life and death
> In a day, so to say—ridiculous!

Ridiculous to live at all
On such a tiny spinning ball!

But these are words, mere words . . .
Let's zoom our minds down, say, in human focus and feel;
Know and feel and see
Our huge, majestic world reel slowly through centuries,
And the great and glorious sun come up slowly,
And the distant, vast hills begin to loom,
Soar and assume dark shapes and sharp edges
Against the pale pink of the sky,
And the high peaks run down in ridges
To the wet, dark, silent valleys below,
Where nothing yet can be known but noises,
Running water and the croak of frogs.

But the world turns,
And pink pales slowly to pearly gold.
And rivers run not nowhere now,
And no longer only murmur in darkness
As if they'd lost their way;
We see.

We see reed beds dimly swaying and dark rocks,
And how the river mist lifts and curls.
As rose to pale gold lost,
So pale gold now to other lightness lifts,
And clouds all mackerel green and grey
Stay steady like a painted scene,
While the clear light of morning blue is set
That declares the scene is day.
What sort of day has dawned for this man
Whom we shall see presently behind this curtain?
Nothing is certain but that dawn begins
And night ends day.
And who among us shall see the next dawn certainly
No man can say.

The first stanza, with its slow and quiet rhythms as we read,
and no doubt even more as we hear it in the crowded theater, acts
upon us almost immediately like a kind of calming hypnosis. Our
minds grow still, our restless bodies settle quietly, all worldly and
irrelevant thoughts sink away; and, in that "dim darkness", we see

what the poet tells us to see—the tiny speck (and how intensely his words make us realize its extreme smallness): ". . . the smallest speck / The tiniest mote or atom it [the mind] can think of—tip and touch / And yet hold some memory of so doing—." The minute speck is "our whole world," spinning senselessly (it seems) in a meaninglessly accidental universe. The next stanza, with its casual-sounding language and unponderous but not indifferent rhythm, reinforces the sense created here of the apparent purposelessness of the universe, reminding us, almost carelessly, that our world is doomed like all the other worlds that have perished before it.

The tone here is miles away from that of the self-pitying young writers of Britain today—the Osbornes and Becketts, the Weskers and Pinters of the modish theater. Manson quietly accepts the fact that our world is doomed. It is, simply, a fact—one of those facts that we have to accept because we have no alternative. Manson indulges in none of the fashionable heroics, no fulminations against God and those who brought us into the world, no stiff upper lip. He merely mentions the fact, emphasizing its queerness from the human point of view.

In the third and fourth stanzas he brings us nearer to the spinning ball. It looks much larger now but still ridiculously unimportant; it seems quite absurd that the millions of swarming, infinitesimal creatures that crawl upon its surface should so feverishly "cling / To life and this atom"—and for so ludicrously short a period: "Ridiculous to live at all / On such a tiny spinning ball!" The smilingly thoughtful, light, spinning rhythm seems to "throw away" the absurdity of it, implying, "It is not tragic; it is not even important."

But in the next three stanzas, as, at the poet's behest, we "zoom our minds down, say, in human focus and feel; / Know and feel and see," by a few vivid touches, he makes us powerfully feel that, true as all this is in a nonhuman perspective, to us it is "words, mere words"; and, as we go on, the compelling power of the poetry makes us realize with wonderful intensity and delight that the purposelessness of it all is utterly unimportant: it is life itself that matters, and it matters overwhelmingly. Now the language paints an entirely different picture from that of the first four stanzas—a picture all the truer because the one *they* paint is true too; we find ourselves stirred, and deeply, unexpectedly moved by the very coexistence of the beauty and importance of life with its insignificance and extreme fragility as it hangs suspended so precariously in the inconceivable infinite.

Manson achieves this here, in the Prologue, by describing, with the peculiar, delicate, intensely lively and tender vividness of which he is capable, the gradual dawn that is to begin Pat Mulholland's Day. The Prologue sets Pat in his eternal setting in the midst of the unimaginable universe of which he is a part, and to which, in a way, he gives a meaning. The play makes one feel that meaning. It *can* be *felt*, though, of course, never at all defined; it can be felt strongly when, in the play, we are made to bathe for awhile, as it were, in reality, the kind of reality that a poet creates, which, though not the same thing as life, nor a substitute for it, makes us much more alive to the actual that we can never fully know.

The Prologue has its own important function in the play by making us thrillingly aware of the wonderful nonhuman life in the midst of which our human lives are set. It may all be blown away one day, "in a white blast," but in the meantime the rhythmic movement of the pre-dawn light and the shapes of the mountains growing clearer in it are grand and glorious; the changing light and color as the earth "reels slowly" toward day are lovely beyond all speech; and there is something, Manson makes us feel, wonderfully touching and exciting in the multitudinous small life going on in the darkness of the valleys: "The wet, dark, silent valleys below,/Where nothing yet can be known but noises,/Running water and the croak of frogs." In the last stanza come the full dawn and the day, which is to show us Pat Mulholland, and to be his last.

The first scene is to open in his studio—he is a sculptor—very early in the morning, when he has just begun to dress. And the last words of the Prologue make us feel suddenly, peculiarly, poignantly anxious for him. We guess that the story will be a moving one, as indeed it is. The whole Prologue that has set the life on this planet so feelingly against the background of eternity has not diminished its importance but has made us realize it with remarkable force of conviction. For as Mrs. Blaiberg put it, the wife of the man who, at the moment of writing, was the world's longest-surviving heart-transplant patient: "The uncertainty of living makes you glad to be alive. Each morning when he wakes, he says 'Oh lovely! Another day' " As the Prologue comes to an end we are

already deeply engaged in this one particular life which we had
never heard of till this moment: it is already very much our concern:

> What sort of day has dawned for this man
> Whom we shall see presently behind this curtain?
> Nothing is certain but that dawn begins
> And night ends day.
> And who among us shall see the next dawn certainly
> No man can say.

III *Poetic Qualities*

The poem is typical of Manson's work at its best in that it all
quivers with delicate life—delicate and yet strong and deep, the
poet's imaginative intelligence being concerned with ultimates,
just as the Tolstoy passage is. This too, in its very different mode,
has a largeness, a deep seriousness of spirit in it. And it is of this
age; for example, the consciousness of scientific discovery is one of
the constituents of its lifeblood. The language, too, is the spoken
language—the undebased language—of today. Manson is, as
Wordsworth says all true poets are, "a man like other men"; his
language is "the language actually used by men,"—used by men,
not by the advertisers, journalists, and best-selling novelists who
exploit the resources of language in order to sell their writing:
and not by the cerebral poetasters, with their "strangulated utterance" and their search for images that will make them appear
original yet "with it," or "literary" yet Laurentian, or otherwise
cast what they regard as a flattering light on their own personalities. A man on the other hand "speaks with [his] own voice"; his
sole concern is to make others see exactly what he means. He is not
afraid, as so many modern writers seem to be, of "being caught
out." Consequently he is direct, natural, and simple. It is certainly
possible, though perhaps unusual, for a very simple and naïve
adult person to be direct, natural, and simple. For a complex and
sophisticated one, especially nowadays, it is a high achievement,
both intellectual and moral.

And when, in poetry, this kind of simplicity is combined with—
to use an old-fashioned and discredited word—poetic "magic," it
cannot fail to give intense delight. Let us briefly consider one
component of the so-called magic, its rhythm, by examining a

small fragment of it: "Let's zoom our minds down, say, in human focus and feel; / Know and feel and see / Our huge, majestic world reel slowly through centuries." . . . The great grand movement of it, and our marvelous expanding vision, exulting in what is happening, are felt in the movement of the lines. "And the great and glorious sun come up slowly, / And the distant, vast hills begin to loom, / Soar and assume dark shapes and sharp edges." . . . The rhythm expands with the glory of the revelation; our sense of its majesty grows as the words create the scene; and as, step by step, light and sight grow clear, that half-unnoticed rhyme in the middle of the line, "loom-assume," makes us aware of something formal happening here that gives the whole movement added grace and power.

Manson's management of dramatic verse reminds one of the student's comment on the balcony scene in *Romeo and Juliet*. "It is so beautiful," she wrote, "that it is almost poetry." This naïve statement is one of the finest compliments ever paid to Shakespeare's dramatic verse. On the speaker, it unconsciously implied, the scene has had the full effect that poetry with all its devices of sound and rhythm is meant to have, and yet the dialogue was so entirely natural that she had not realized that any devices were being used. This is exactly what T. S. Eliot in his famous essay on dramatic verse said he himself was trying to achieve. In passages like this one from the Prologue to *Pat Mulholland's Day*, the poetic "measure" (to use the old-fashioned term) is never obvious; nevertheless, it is there, part of the "magic." It is there, silently performing the function that Coleridge, Wordsworth, and Eliot among them say that poetic rhythm should perform: it is not only helping to express, by a kind of imitation, the emotion, the passion felt and to be conveyed; it is also controlling and containing it; it is alerting the hearer to the fact that this is not prose but something more important; and it is, by the rhythm of stressed syllables and echoed sounds in it, having the effect of a narcotic which lulls to sleep what is mundane and irrelevant in our minds so as to give greater freedom to what is relevant and vital.

Now, all traditional verse has two rhythms interacting on each other, the one fixed and regular (the meter, for example, iambic pentameter) and the other free (what is usually called the rhythm). In the kind of verse that Manson writes, another kind of rhythm takes the place of the fixed and formal meter of traditional verse, the beat of which is heard like a barely audible drum beat, as it were, underlying the free and flexible rhythmic movements of the second rhythm, which imitate what is being described or expressed. This underlying drum beat in Manson's kind of verse is not insistent, and it is not regular, but it is felt to be there. It is made up of assonances and alliterations and occasional rare rhymes and mid-rhymes (as rare as in *Lycidas,* for example), which make themselves heard like the louder throb of a distant drum. We have *zoom-loom-assume,* in the lines above, and elsewhere, *see-be, away-day, night-light, all-ball, sky-high, grey-day, green-seen, day-say.* Together these rare rhymes, the assonances, and the alliterations make up a subtle and rather irregular pattern, much more evident to the ear than to the eye—a pattern which underlies the imitative rhythm and is just sufficently formal to have the threefold effect—the "magic" which Wordsworth, Coleridge, and Eliot speak of, and which one feels so strongly in this Prologue.

Manson's language in the Prologue is very close to that of the dialogue in his play, for though only one man is speaking here, he is not soliloquizing but speaking directly to someone—to the audience. The difference between the language here and that of exchanges of speech between the dramatis personae is that their speech is very much affected by their characters and by the action, the mood, and the genre of each particular play.

The use of this kind of simple language, so like ordinary speech and yet not quite ordinary speech, and this kind of verse form, so like prose, and yet decidedly not prose, is one of the marks of Manson's originality, for it is his own spontaneous invention. I cannot think of any other playwright who uses verse like this— who has broken away from blank verse or the heroic couplet, neither of which seems to suit our modern speech rhythms, and writes natural dialogue which is nevertheless poetry—has all the effect of poetry, and yet does not create a barrier of strangeness between the play and its modern audience. This kind of thing is also a sign of his being a born dramatist. When two of Manson's plays were sent to that great and experienced actor, Sir Ralph Richardson, he commented on the beauty of the poetry and the fact that the writer had "a strong feeling for the theatre," and "a real understanding of dialogue." Mr. John Duncan Macrae, said to be the best actor on the Scottish stage, expressed a similar admiration for the poetic beauty of the language and the instinct for dialogue and "theatre."

These slight comments will serve, I hope, to hint to our readers, both overseas and at home, that London is not at present the place to look in for new and original dramatic writing—for drama which, though in no way derivative, yet belongs, as Dr. Leavis says the great American novels, such as those of Mark Twain and Nathaniel Hawthorne do, to the great tradition of English literature and drama. In the "swinging" London of today, the mass media seem to be making true originality and even artistic sanity impossible. But, judging by this one case (and South Africa has yielded other writers of merit), in the remoter and as yet not overpopulated regions of the English-speaking world, originality and sanity are still, though extremely rare, at least possible; and we hope in the rest of this book to do something toward justifying this thesis.

CHAPTER 2

Biography

I *Ancestry and Early Life*

A fostering childhood is perhaps partly what has enabled Manson to survive, as a writer, the frustrations of living in an age hostile to his most valuable qualities. In dealing very briefly with Manson's life, I shall leave out all reference to what is merely personal. A writer's personal life is strictly his own concern, and most of those who inquire into it are indulging, not in scholarship, as the world seems to believe, but in the questionable pleasures of gossip, or in amateur psychoanalysis at a disabling remove. I shall, therefore, apart from a few bare facts, speak only of his background, and tell one or two anecdotes illustrative of his inventiveness and dramatic bent.

Manson's ancestors were, on the father's side, partly Scandinavian but chiefly Scottish; on the mother's, Scandinavian. His grandfather was from the Shetland Islands and used to talk, he fully believed, to ghosts; the family all seem to have been born with strongly marked personalities. At the time of Manson's birth, his father, having fought in the 1914 war in the Southwest-African campaign, was settled on the African continent, where he had become an electrical engineer in the British Colonial Service in Tanganyika (now Tanzania). There Manson was born, January 29, 1926, in the little town of Tabora. He was the youngest of three children, Leonard, Audrey (called Winkey) and Harley (that is, H.W.D.).

In Tabora the family lived for nine years. Childhood in the Manson household must have been remarkably spacious, free, and adventurous, as childhood could be in the "outposts of empire" in those days, but it was not without discipline. The children were all fearless. "I think I did teach my children courage," says their mother. When the children fought, among themselves, and with the African and English boys, they fought wholeheartedly to win, observing no Queensberry rules. They hated a half-hearted approach to anything. Manson despised people who could not put their whole selves into work or games or fighting. He could be ruthless in his insistence on courage in everything: it is a universal duty, a virtue which it is shameful to lack. Though profoundly compassionate by nature, he had nevertheless no patience with "petty unselfishness," "coddled sensibilities," and "exaggerated solicitudes." *

The family members were all warmhearted, quick-tempered, and unconventional, with a passion for animals and all living things. And there were strange wild creatures where they lived. In Tabora they had a pet warthog, called Binty Marufu. Warthogs to most people are extraordinarily ugly: in the Mansons' animal-loving eyes, they are "charming." Binty Marufu used to sleep on the living-room sofa. Once, having crept under the kitchen stove for warmth, she arose in the morning with the stove on her back. And there were lions, even commoner then than now, and other beasts of prey in that world. Manson's mother, appreciating, like her children, the lion's point of view as well as her own, tells several stories about them. For example, one wet, stormy night, a missionary friend built a big fire in her living room. All at once, in the midst of buckets of rain, constant lightning, and crashing thunder, she heard a loud thumping on the front door. A wayfarer, come for refuge, she thought. She opened the door. Fortunately it opened inward, so that she remained behind it against the wall, for who should walk in but a huge black-maned lion, dripping wet and miserable! He had been lashing his tail against the door. The missionary froze, flattened against the wall; unaware of her, the lion appeared to welcome the blazing fire, for he walked straight to the hearth, shook himself all over like a big dog till he was nearly dry, then lay down on the hearthrug, stretched himself out, and soon, to the onlooker's huge relief fell fast asleep. Still as a mouse, she crept along the wall till she came to another door, quietly opened it, then locked it from the other side, locked all the inside doors, and warned the household. They spent a night of terror, until, at dawn, the storm having ceased, the lion woke up and walked off quietly home again.

On another dark night in Tanganyika several young men were

* The first phrase is from E. M. Forster, the other two from Henry James.

sitting in a bedroom, when they heard their host in the garden shouting in a high and startled voice, "What are *you* doing here! How dare you come into my garden! Get out at once! Get out!" and so on. He was addressing a leopard, and sheer fright had produced the indignant words. The leopard, too, was startled, for he made off without delay.

Those were the days, especially in the colonies, of many servants. Each of the children when small had his own particular African body servant, whose business it was to look after his special charge, often telling him wise and fascinating stories from African lore, and incidentally teaching him good manners and good morals, and checking and even punishing him when he behaved badly. The family all spoke Swahili, and there was mutual liking and respect. There was one man whose sole function it was to turn the handle of the old-fashioned gramophone, and there is a family photograph with him proudly holding up the gramophone handle, honorable symbol of his office. This kind of master-servant relationship is no bad thing, so long as it is not made too difficult for members of the servant class to rise to higher rank, even the highest. Certainly, on the average, relationships of this kind may make for more interesting and varied lives than many people realize, with stronger human interests on both sides of the line, each regarding the other's family as, in a way, his own, and genuinely participating in joys and sorrows that they would otherwise not share. In fact, a society of this kind may be good soil for the basic human virtues to grow in, and is a good nursery for the young creative mind. One cannot live as a child in wilder Africa, and grow up imagining that life and people are really as Wesker and Pinter and Beckett represent them.

II *Residence in England*

In 1933, the worst year of the great depression, the Manson family went to England on leave. Mr. Manson, like so many other colonial civil servants, was retrenched and, after nine months on pension, accepted a post in the Bahamas. There he remained, while Mrs. Manson took first a caravan and then a house in Ramsgate for the children. In the caravan they spent a pleasant year traveling all over England; the house was large and roomy, with a big garden, and the children were sent to school, Manson to Chatham House in Ramsgate. In this school his elder brother,

Leonard, and Edward Heath, four years Leonard's senior, acted together in one or two Aldwych farces.

Even in England the children lived a largely outdoor life, swimming in the sea, walking, cycling, climbing in the country, and scrambling about; they were wild creatures whom the polite English boys did not understand. They read voraciously, especially the future poet, in history, travel, war, biography, poetry, drama. Manson's memory was always remarkably retentive, which partly accounts for the astonishing quantity of general out-of-the-way knowledge which this man who disliked intensely the academic world and everything that smells of the lamp had accumulated.

In 1939 the Ramsgate house was sold, and at Christmas, three months after the outbreak of war, Mrs. Manson and the children moved to Johannesburg—except for Leonard, who had had a year's military training at Sandhurst, and had enlisted almost immediately. Manson was sent to school in the famous Saint Andrew's College in Grahamstown, South Africa. There he spent several tempestuous years, being beaten literally every day and, on one memorable day, when he had started off by meaning to be particularly good, no less than four times.

Manson's stories of his school days were full of the bright, tantalizing, satirical humor which often delighted even when it exasperated his victims. But even at that early age he possessed the poet's habit and gift of intently observing his fellows; his stories showed that he must have had a degree of compassionate insight most unusual in young boys. The insight had no doubt been deepened and enriched retrospectively—but tears were sometimes brought to the listener's eye by his tales of some school fellow or master, perhaps long dead—killed in the last war, most likely, for Saint Andrew's has always been a patriotic school, bound to ancestral Britain. One story concerns a school fellow in England, who, though able and clever, was so clumsy that he was physically almost an imbecile: he was always falling over his own feet, could not run, and was hopelessly bad at all sports. Manson, being especially strong, active, and nimble, was asked to take him in hand, and, by sheer patience and concentrated interest, he managed to teach him a modicum of physical skill. A few years later, however, this boy, then a man, was killed in World War II. One evening, not very many years ago, Manson was driving along not very far from Pietermaritzburg in the dusk. He was utterly exhausted and was in great danger of falling asleep at the wheel. Presently he became aware of his dead friend sitting beside him in the front of the car. The friend suggested that they should stop the car, get out, and go for a walk. This they did, walking and talking together in the gathering darkness. After awhile Manson found himself alone and refreshed. He went back to the car and continued the journey in safety. This story is not for the Psychical Research Society. The experience was produced, most likely, by the action upon a mind naturally creative of a number of things: a half-conscious sense of danger; an affectionate and intensely imaginative, though almost unconscious, memory of a personality; and a mind too exhausted to distinguish illusion from reality.

III   War Years

After sitting for the matriculation exam at the end of 1943, Manson, then seventeen, without waiting for the results, enlisted; after training he was posted to the Natal Carbineers, with whom he served in Italy in 1944 and 1945.

Both Manson and his brother Leonard told enthralling and sometimes hair-raising stories from their inexhaustible store of tales about the 1939–45 war. From others and from each other one heard of their exceptional courage. Leonard, the elder by six years, won the Military Cross, but apart from that, was noted for always volunteering for the most dangerous jobs, like raiding a sleeping enemy camp in the small hours, with one or two companions, and bringing back a prisoner for interrogation. Since he too had a humane and imaginative nature, he told his younger brother that sometimes to that day when he thought of some exploit he had volunteered for, the cold sweat would break out on his forehead. Neither brother could understand how any young man could deliberately pass over the chance of war experience. Manson, though utterly free from the nonsense of "living dangerously" by indulging in perversion, drug-taking, and the like, yet never refused a personal challenge or avoided the need for manly action; certainly, the ultimate experiences of war bore fruit in the firsthand knowledge of life on which his plays are based.

IV *Further Education*

When the war was over, safely for both of them, the young men returned to their mother's flat in Johannesburg, at first in rather restless mood. (Both their mother and their sister Winkey had also contributed to the Allied war effort.) Leonard followed something of a family tradition by joining the British Colonial Service as an assistant commissioner; he later became a district commissioner and served in Nigeria, Tanganyika, and Bechuanaland, as they then were. But Manson decided to continue his education and enrolled at the University of the Witwatersrand, Johannesburg, where in due course he took a degree in English and fine art, for both of which he had exceptional talent. He had not only extremely unusual gifts as a writer but also had a strong leaning toward the plastic arts; as a child he used to love molding animals in clay; and to his last year he liked to draw with his fountain pen—delicate, lively line drawings of animals, full of movement and character, human figures, and lightning characterizations (not caricatures) of people. His first idea, he has said, was to be a painter, and the painter's habit of looking at everything carefully and with pleasure has entered very considerably into his writing.

I have in my possession to this day the fruit of a delightful invention of Manson's which illustrates both the talent for drawing and that for dramatic characterization. This fruit is a sheet of foolscap on which, apropos of someone nicknamed "Horse," he had begun by giving me an example of "Horse-writing," then "Crab-writing," "Fly-writing," "Moth-writing," etc., followed by a delicately executed line of each, each somehow a convincing expression of the kind of creature that was supposed to have written it. Presently this developed into a disquisition on Fish Poetry, with examples. (The examples are on the paper too.) There are, apparently, a special language and special rules of rhythm and rhyme for Fish Poetry. As it went on, the disquisition was being delivered by a particular individual of Manson's invention, a professor of insect graphology in Egypt, whose sideline was Fish Poetry—an extremely erudite character, an English gentleman from Oxford (not caricatured, but taken respectfully), very precise and with exquisite taste, but perhaps a little precious.

The ex-servicemen's university classes just after the war were most interesting to teach (I was lecturing at "Wits" at the time). One felt about the best of these men that they were not going to go meekly into any kind of job that offered them "security." They had known plenty of insecurity, and they had seen life and death; they were highly critical, and they had matured rapidly. They were men, and they had a strong sense of reality. When I first knew Manson there was still a certain deceptive softness about his features; with his bright gold hair, his bright blue eyes, and a remarkable look of physical power and liveliness about his whole rather stocky person, almost as if vitality were visibly streaming from him in rays, he reminded one of Perdita's phrase, "bright Phoebus in his strength." A year or two later he grew a bright gold beard, and this strengthened the impression.

The appearance of vitality, which he maintained throughout his life, did not belie him. He was the most inventive person most of his acquaintances had ever met. The family still tell a story of him as a little boy of ten or eleven, which is known as "The Canterbury Lie." One morning in Ramsgate he went off on his bicycle to play with a friend. He was to have been home by lunchtime, but the boys were enjoying themselves so much that when the friend's mother asked Harley to stay to lunch, he did so. In due course teatime came; after more hours of absorption, suppertime, and each time he yielded to the temptation to stay. At length it was bedtime, and he was persuaded to share his friend's bedroom. It was not till late the next day that he decided to cycle home to his distracted parents. They were quite mollified when the little boy told them that he had decided to go to look at Canterbury Cathedral and city and described everything that he had done and seen in the thirty-six hours—where he had spent the night, how he had got food and what he had eaten, all in minute and vivid detail. The family were delighted with his enterprise and originality in going so far and seeing so much all by himself at his tender age, and it was some days before the mine was exploded under him and the Canterbury lie blown to pieces.

V   Personality; Dramatic Inventiveness

The Canterbury story illustrates his native gift for narrative and drama. It is illustrated even better by his practice when he went mountain climbing with his friend David Gillham (also an ex-